COSTING
THE EARTH

Ronald Banks, Editor

SHEPHEARD-WALWYN
in association with

CENTRE FOR INCENTIVE TAXATION

© 1989 Centre for Incentive Taxation
177 Vauxhall Bridge Road
London SW1V 1EU

This edition first published 1989 by
Shepheard-Walwyn (Publishers) Ltd
26 Charing Cross Road (Suite 34)
London WC2H 0DH

ISBN 0 85683 111 5

Typeset by Alacrity Phototypesetters,
Banwell Castle, Weston-super-Mare
Printed and bound in Great Britain by
Cox and Wyman Ltd, Reading, Berkshire

Acknowledgements

THE AUTHORS received the generous advice of many experts, some of whom requested anonymity. Thanks are particularly extended to V. H. Blundell, Chris Bryant, Geoff Clarke, Alice Coleman, Richard Fordham, T. Hardie, St. John Hartnell, David Little, Joe Martin, Ron O'Regan, Syd Price, Andy Prokop, Janet Shaw, Mike Skaife, Charles Smart, Jimmy Walker, Peter Walls, Nick Ward and Hector Wilks. None of them is responsible for any errors that may be contained in this study, the responsibility for which rests with the authors; nor should they be regarded as endorsing the conclusions arising out of the enquiry into a politically most sensitive issue.

Contents

Foreword

POLITICAL economy is at the crossroads. Its practitioners, from the point of view of public policy, are no nearer to articulating solutions to the disturbing booms and slumps which compromise the right of men and women to achieve their aspirations.

The two economic systems of the world now also face difficult choices, for neither has survived the test of time unscathed. The leaders of the Marxist-based societies have effectively thrown in the towel; no longer do they champion the command economy with any sense of conviction. The hypnotic powers of Hegelian metaphysics have not withstood the gaze of *glasnost*. But this offers little comfort to the leaders of the Western market economies, for it was the defects in the capitalist system that spawned the experiment in socialism. Those structural defects have yet to be corrected, a fact which continues to provide comfort to the advocates of the 'mixed' economy.

These are exciting times, then, for theory and practice can now converge on a new path.

The authors of this volume do not share the general cynicism which, understandably, is now directed at the science of political economy. They believe that the foundation principles articulated by the classical economists, if logically and honestly employed, offer the guides that would release people from the material constraints on their lives which persist despite the progress of the last two centuries.

If we were to seek a point in time when things started to go badly wrong, it was during the dying years of the 19th century. The theory of economics underwent a fundamental change that was more radical than is generally appreciated. The essential character of that transformation was a simple one of definition.

In the West, the concept of land — broadly defined to include all the resources of nature — was subordinated into a sub-species of capital. The clarity of the theory of rent was obscured. The consequences were far-reaching; policy-makers lost one of the main analytical tools at their disposal.

Simultaneously, Marx set the course for the East by emphasising the primacy of the labour and capital markets. For practical purposes, the rental value of land was banished by the labour theory of value.

The time has now come to retrieve the theory of rent from its obscurity and re-affirm the role of nature in the destiny of mankind. Whether this will be enough to set the science of political economy on a firmer foundation, and lead to the articulation of a sustainable social and economic order, only time will tell. But one thing seems to be certain: the environmental crises that now confront the world cannot be sensibly analysed and resolved without the application of the classical theory of rent.

The challenge will not be sidestepped, if for no other reason than that the ecological imperatives will impact on the political process and the balance of international power in a fundamental way. The realisation of this fact is already compelling statesmen to reappraise the future with a new sense of urgency. Nature, in a very real sense, is setting the agenda for the remainder of this century.

It is towards a renewed interest in the way in which we use — and abuse — the resources of nature that this book is dedicated. The authors suspect that this will lead to a rent in the veil of ignorance that has hitherto shrouded the process of policy formation, and so direct us to a new approach, one that is capable of balancing conflicting interests into something like the ideal system of harmony originally envisaged by the classical economists.

RONALD BANKS
London, March 1989

PART ONE

1

Ecology, Politics and the Nature of Rent

FRED HARRISON

HOW MUCH rent should be paid by people occupying the ozone layer with the byproducts of their aerosols and refrigerators? If a rent had been payable, the greenhouse effect might not be threatening a global crisis. The notion of placing a value on the benefits of employing this stratospheric layer of 'land' — broadly defined by economists to include all of nature's freely-given resources — is only unrealistic because the ozone layer protects life from exposure to dangerous levels of ultra-violet radiation. It is a critical part of the life-protecting ecological system, and therefore priceless. The only sensible action, in this case, is to forgo the rent and forbid anyone from occupying the space with the chlorofluorocarbons (CFCs) which inflict damage on the delicate chemistry of the ozone layer and heighten the risk of skin cancer.

But the principle of properly valuing the resources of nature and requiring users to adopt a responsible attitude towards man's common inheritance by paying for the privilege of using it now confronts the world's statesmen as the most difficult — and critical — political challenge before them. For the failure to make people pay rent for access to, or possession of, natural resources is at the heart of all major environmental problems, and is the cause of some of the most fractious geo-political confrontations.

The problem is most readily perceived at the local level, where we can see how rivers and seas are seriously polluted because users are not compelled to pay the full cost for occupying the water with their wastes. Put another way, the problem arises because the community is not properly compensated for allowing polluters to

3

use its ecological habitat. This anomalous situation is not peculiar to a particular socio-economic system. It manifests itself in societies where resources are equally owned by, and theoretically available to, everyone, as well as in countries where land is privately owned to the exclusion of those who do not have their names on title deeds.

In the command economies of Eastern Europe property rights are vested in the State. In the Soviet Union, the phenomenal waste of natural resources over the six decades following the revolution is the direct result of the application of Marx's labour theory of value, which led the Communist Party to treat land as having no value because it had no cost of production. Rent, therefore, was not charged for its use. Its vast regions of virgin soil were exploited extensively in a process that successfully dissipated a large amount of labour and capital, as well as land. The process originated with Stalin's murderous programme of collectivisation, the destruction of the peasant's relationship with the fields and the over-taxation of rural incomes to finance socialist industrialisation. Mikhail Gorbachev's attempt to turn back the pages of history, by enabling peasants to farm more efficiently on plots held under lease, is aimed at raising productivity and enabling the USSR to feed its citizens. But 'in a country where there has been no proper price on land, working out lease contracts is tricky,' noted *The Economist* on March 11, 1989, six days before the Party's Central Committee approved the adoption of the leasehold system of private farming.

Without an accurate pricing mechanism, either the leasehold system will not work or the new kulaks will gain an advantage, through the privatisation of rental income. This has already happened in China. Some peasants have become disproportionately rich because of the failure to measure the full rental value of land and charge for its possession and use. This makes a mockery of the State's claim that it continues to own the title deeds to the land.

Ironically, the Western market economies are almost as guilty, even though property rights are owned by individuals who are supposed to jealously husband their assets. Here, as we shall see, it is the exercise of monopoly power that distorts the price and allocation of land and encourages the wilful waste.

The Valuation of Land

A new approach, if it can be devised, has to start with an inventory of all natural resources and an accurate assessment of current market values. But according to some experts it is not possible to single out land for valuation purposes, especially the sites in urban locations. This view is expressed by eminent scholars, among them Donald Denman, the former professor of land economics at the University of Cambridge, and is articulated by James Boubright, a professor in the United States, in *The Valuation of Property, a Treatise on the Appraisal of Property for Different Legal Purposes* (Vol. 1: 485):

> Although a separate valuation of land and of improvements is called for by many of the statutes as well as by practice of assessors, the fictitious nature of this separation is apparent. One simply cannot find the value — by adding the value of the ground devoid of the building, to the value of the building devoid of the ground.

If correct, this suggests a bleak future. It implies a continuation of the profligate use of finite resources, with increasingly ominous implications for both the natural environment and international relations.

The perplexing aspect of the Boubright thesis is that property developers, and their professional advisers, routinely separate the value of land from buildings. The objection that this cannot be realistically executed transforms economics into metaphysics. This is exemplified by Boubright's illustration. Separating the value of land from the value of buildings, he claims, would be to commit the same error as would occur 'were we to seek the value of Raphael's "Sistine Madonna" by adding the separate value of the lower half of the canvas to the separate value of the upper half.'

In the United States, one can regularly photograph families jacking up their homes — the structures — on to the backs of lorries and trundling them away to other locations. They built (or paid someone else to build) those houses, whereas the land was not manufactured and is fixed permanently *in situ*, provided free by nature. The house depreciates in value, as it ages, while land appreciates in value as the community around it expands. Yet some authorities still seriously maintain that the value of a piece of real estate — land, and buildings on it — is a homogeneous whole, in the way that a painting is 'of a piece'.

This represents the rent of land as somehow just beyond the intellectual grasp of mortals, and leaves the impression of unfinished business that must one day be sorted out, perhaps in more reflective times. This attitude might not matter if it did not impinge on the business of public policy formation, but it does. For example:

> Because land, unlike financial assets, is not homogeneous, the market value cannot be unambiguously defined, complicating the task of taxing land fairly (OECD 1988: 77).

The nebulous character of this reasoning reflects the low interest in the economics of land. There are rationalised explanations for this neglect. For example, Dr. Bill Robinson (then of the London Business School) explaining why trends in the level of rents did not feature in his analysis of the UK economy in 1983, wrote this: 'I did not include rent in my analysis for the good reason that rents, for the economy as a whole, have not grown especially rapidly over the period. Moreover there are good theoretical reasons for excluding rents: high rents are in general a symptom of success, not a cause of failure'.[1]

Had it been considered worthwhile investigating rent as a share of the UK's income, the marked increase that manifested itself in the second half of the 1980s might have been predicted. The value of urban rental income doubled between 1985 and 1988. The reply to this, however, might be: 'So what?' For on the orthodox view, any acceleration in the rate of growth of rents is no more than a measure of economic prosperity. The rent of land (as we shall see) is a surplus income. Under certain strict assumptions, it is true that an increase in this surplus income reflects the successful expansion of the rate of growth of the economy without implying any dysfunctional side-effects.

But what happens if that trend in rents is in part generated either by imperfections in the land market, or by other motives (such as a disposition to speculate in land)? In such an event, there is a risk that rental income might outpace the growth of incomes received

Figure 1 : I
Growth of urban land rent and income from
employment and self-employment 1985-1990

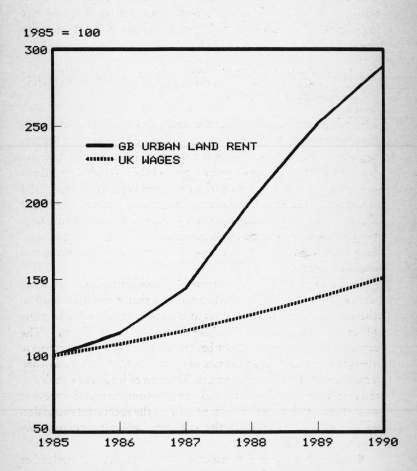

1985 = 100

GB URBAN LAND RENT

UK WAGES

Source: As in Table 1 : II

by employees for their work or by entrepreneurs on their investments. Theoretically, this could generate the possibility of a
distortion in consumption and investment, which is what occurred
in 1988/9. House prices in Britain rose by well over 30% p.a., while
income from employment rose by under 10%. Over the last half
of the decade, the value of urban land rents as a percentage of
national income nearly doubled. Income from employment and self
employment as a percentage of national income remained almost
constant.[2] The bifurcation in the income trends (Fig. 1:I) had
maleficent implications for homeowners, who had to sacrifice a
great deal to finance their mortgages. Earnings failed to keep pace
with the rate of increase in the cost of houses (more precisely, the
rapid rise in the price of residential land). This caused social and
economic stresses such as homelessness, over-crowding and labour
immobility, the evidence for which should modify the complacent
view that a rapid increase in rents is necessarily an index of success.[3]

The Unique Factor

For practical purposes the valuation of land presents no problems
for the professional: even so, we agree that the essential nature of
the rent of land does display a certain elusive quality. The conceptual difficulties, however, dissolve once terms are used in a consistent manner.[4]

Land as a factor of production is unique, which therefore makes
rent in some sense special. The stream of income known as economic rent is a surplus, in that it is not part of the costs of
producing goods or services. In other words, the rent accruing to
land is the difference between the costs of production and the
revenue a business receives from customers. To qualify as land rent,
this income must exclude the returns to the undepreciated capital
— buildings and other man-made improvements — expended on
land.

The notion that rent is not a cost of production may seem
paradoxical to people who enter rent into their ledgers as a cost that
has to be met if they are to remain as tenants on their landlord's
premises. These facts of life disguise the nature of rent.

The rental value of land is a measure of the benefits that stem from the use of particular sites. To occupy an acre of land near its customers means that a firm's transport costs are lower than those of its competitor further afield, even though both charge the same prices for similar products. The difference in haulage costs — the savings enjoyed by the occupier of the land near the market — is not retained as higher profits, or paid out in higher wages, but is incorporated by the owner into the price of the site. This element of the land's rental value is a measure of *lower* marketing costs; it expresses the *saving* that accrues to the occupier of the fortuitously-located site.

The transformation of part of a firm's aggregate income into rent is neatly illuminated by the residual method of valuation.

Developers calculate the cost of construction, including the profits they require on the capital they are laying out on the building and other improvements to the site. They then compare these costs with the price they can expect to achieve by selling (or renting out) the building. The costs are subtracted from the revenue and the difference (the surplus) is the amount claimed by the landowner. The acquisition of a site may be the first practical step in the physical construction of a building, but it is only taken by a prudent businessman *after* he has calculated the revenue he can expect to receive, so that he knows how much will be left over once all his costs have been met. Only then can he talk turkey with the landowner.

This economic process is reflected in the application of the law for property tax purposes in the United States. Sec. 502(3) of New York State's Real Property Tax Law requires the assessor first to value the land exclusive of improvements on it, and then arrive at a total assessed value. The assessor is not required to value the building *per se*. 'To arrive at a total value he takes his land value and includes whatever increment the building adds to the land,' according to Horace Z. Kramer, writing as the counsel to the New York State Assembly Standing Committee on Real Property Taxation (*New York Times*, Nov. 15, 1983). Kramer adds, by way of illustrating that the tenets of jurisprudence are consonant with day-to-day realities:

The marketplace proves this method works. Where the land by itself becomes so valuable that the building does not add to its value, the building is demolished and a new one constructed which will maximize the value of the land. Where, in blighted areas, the buildings are not productive, the value of the property is in the land only, less the cost of demolition.

Kramer errs in suggesting that a new building 'will maximize the value of the land'. The land has already acquired the value by virtue of its location in relation to the current needs of the community, as expressed by the rent people are willing to pay for it. Erecting the appropriate building on the site to meet those needs is merely the first stage in releasing the full value.

Markets and Monopoly

Academic economists persist in the view that high rents are a symptom of success (and therefore uninteresting for the purpose of measurement and further research), although they know that this is true only under conditions of perfect competition. What are the specifications of their theory? We are interested in two of them. First, the prospective users of land have to enjoy access to full information, so that they can make rational decisions. Second, individual landowners are assumed to accept the passive role of price takers who lack the power to regulate the market to their advantage.

If these conditions apply, the level of rents is not a problem for the efficient user of land. As prices rise and fall in response to the pressures of a dynamic economy (shifts in demand, as consumer tastes change; technological progress, which cuts costs; product innovation, and so on), the surplus (land rent) responsively diminishes or increases.

The land market, according to the postulates of this theory, is submissive, and cannot interfere with the myriad decisions taken by producers and consumers. It receives the left-overs, after labour and capital have been paid off for doing their job of satisfying the consumers.

Unfortunately, under the present system of tenure and taxation, land is not used and traded in a perfectly competitive market. Property owners are not forced by competition into docility. They enjoy the power to make decisions which can distort competition. They can consequently intervene in the productive process and, to an extent, they can *determine* the level of rents in particular sub-markets. An important feature of this power is the right to withhold land from potential users. This is an easily verified assertion: one only needs to drive through the heart of a city to observe the number of valuable acres that lie vacant despite the existence of unsatisfied demand for their use. By diminishing supply, the landowner alters the relative values of the remaining sites.

It is important to be aware that landowners, in exercising their power, are not directly forcing up the price of goods and services by reducing the supply of available land and driving up the level of rents. Rents are not a cost of production and they therefore do not enter into the price-fixing process.[5] The impact on the economy, however, limits the employment and production prospects. Firms that might have been commercially viable, in that their services could just be marketed at a bare but acceptable profit, find themselves unable to generate sufficient surplus to satisfy the landlord. Because of competition in their market, they cannot unilaterally raise prices to meet the demands of landowners. Since the landlord is not a price-taker, he evicts his tenants, who are relegated to the marginal hinterland. There, they go bust, taking with them the jobs that would otherwise have kept some people fruitfully employed.

This is not the outcome of collective meanness by landowners, but the logic of an economic system that grants to the owners of natural resources the privilege of being able to withdraw from competition. Property rights and the tax system do not require owners to account for their possession of land. On the contrary, as we shall see, the reverse is true: they are often provided with incentives that appear to be wilfully designed to persuade owners *not* to use their land. Whatever the motive, the outcome is unambiguous: the arrogation to some people of a power of monopoly over natural resources, which successfully undermines the efficiency of the market economy.

This identification of land markets with monopoly power is not readily accepted by free market economists such as Frederick

Hayek and Milton Friedman, who observe that property rights in land are diffused among thousands, even millions of people. Their attitude is shaped by the neo-classical definition of monopoly, which entails the collusion of a few people or corporations to rig a market in their favour and at the customer's expense. But this is one example only of a monopoly situation.

Far more important is the concept developed by the classical economists. They focused on the means by which a barrier could be erected to bar entry into a market. Such a barrier is most damagingly associated with non-reproducible natural resources, the engrossment of which

> on the first-come first-served basis ... denies to future generations access to these productive resources on the same terms as the first generation. What [Adam] Smith, J. S. Mill, and [Henry] George clearly meant when they spoke of land rent as a monopoly return was that land owned by one person cannot be reproduced by his competitors at its (zero) original real cost of production (Dwyer 1982: 367).

This concept of a barrier also entails the literal meaning. Landowners can, and do, prevent prospective users from gaining access to their sites, which limits production to the disadvantage of consumers. The 'No Trespassing' warning nailed to the fence is philosophically treated as a sign of the liberty of the individual, but little thought is devoted in the Lockean tradition to the possibility that it may also signify the negation of the life and liberty of the outsider.

In the communist countries, economic necessity is leading to a fundamental review of theories of property rights; in the capitalist countries, the debate will commence once we understand that the ecological costs of economic success are threatening the natural habitat. A starting point for any review of property rights has to be the thorough assembly of all information about the price of land and a new interest in how the market operates.

The Politicisation of Rent

Politicians have a singularly important influence over the distribution of rental income. That this should be so is not surprising, for politics are at the root of property in land. Original rights of tenure derive from appropriation, not through saving, investment or production. It may therefore be correct for society, through the political process, to influence the manner in which land is used and the way in which the benefits are distributed. But if so, the process ought to be an open one; generally, it isn't. The political influences are almost entirely secretive. This contrasts in a stark way with the manner in which politicians seek to influence the labour and capital markets.

For macro-economic purposes, governments regularly pass laws and implement grand strategies to raise or lower profits of capital and wages of labour; they never declare their *intention* to alter the price of land. Entrepreneurs are encouraged to increase productivity through new capital investment, and inducements are offered ranging from special subsidies to lower taxes. Employees are exhorted to work harder, and governments use a variety of stick-and-carrot inducements to encourage the appropriate responses. Landowners are never lectured. And yet politicians do, as a matter of routine, exercise power that has far-reaching consequences on rent.

Analysis of the impact of governmental decisions on natural resources is of paramount importance, yet it cannot be satisfactorily undertaken because of the paucity of the most basic of information, such as trends in the price of land and the quantities that are being traded at any given time. Astonishingly, there is even a general absence of interest in the dynamics of the land market itself. One consequence is that, shrouded in what for all practical purposes is a mantle of mystery, the land market operates in a way which is not always consistent with the policy goals of government.

There is nothing novel about the statement that Governments routinely redistribute people's incomes. When the tax laws are changed, or special fiscal provisions are written onto the statute books, some citizens gain while others lose. In a democracy, this is acceptable; for by definition, everyone has had a right to express his or her views on the general thrust of policy through the ballot box. So when a government raises taxes from one section of the community, thereby reducing their living standards, for the sake of spending money on, say, health care or education for the poor, the process is at least subject to democratic scrutiny.

By contrast, there is a class of government actions which is concealed from public examination yet entails a massive redistribution of income. As a byproduct of their decisions on other issues, governments redistribute income both within the land market and as between land, labour and capital, while rarely being called to account. These decisions enhance or diminish the financial status of property owners, but unless they involve the clearest acts of 'taking,' as it is called in the United States, the owners have little chance of receiving compensation for the loss of the rental value of their land; conversely, the landowners who gain — the usual case — are rarely required to relinquish their windfall profits.

The covert manner by which some landowners are regaled with riches is rarely subjected to scrutiny, yet the most fundamental consequences flow from the political deeds. For example, until the Chancellor of the Exchequer changed the rules in the 1988 budget, Britain provided attractive tax incentives to people willing to invest in forests. The intention was to encourage the growth of more timber, but part of the financial inducements were capitalised into higher prices for land. It was this opportunity, not the desire to become foresters, which persuaded pop stars and TV talk-show hosts to invest their money in vast tracts of Scottish land. The money was effectively being ploughed into the selective pockets of tax havens within the British Isles.

The same process is at work in agriculture, where farmers are heavily protected from the disciplines of the market place by various price support and trade-obstructing measures. This reduces the living standards of consumers while enhancing the financial benefits absorbed by the land owners. According to Sir Richard Body, a farmer and Conservative Member of Parliament, in the 36-year period following 1946 the taxpayers and consumers were required by successive British governments to plough £40,000m in subsidies of one sort or another into agriculture. In this period, he estimated the increase in land values at £40,000m (Body 1982: 20, 32).

These outcomes were not intended by the government, but the subterranean process by which part of the flow of income is capitalised into higher land values results in the impoverishment of one group and the enrichment of another. This is never the goal of public policy. Rather, governments say they want the nation to be less dependent upon timber imports, or that they wish to provide working farmers with higher living standards. Instead, revenue that was supposed to fulfil these purposes is leaked away into rent for the owners of a resource whose contribution to the process of production is nil. The deleterious impact does not stop there, moreover, for the higher rents serve as a barrier that obstructs newcomers who want to enter the industry. This successfully limits competition, raises prices, probably diminishes efficiency and certainly reduces the benefits that would otherwise accrue to consumers.

The transfer of income is concealed by both the failure to monitor the trends in the value of land, and the absence of a meaningful debate about the way in which the land market operates. The appeal for more information about the market, then, is not a frivolous one. The availability of full information is a precondition for an efficient market; its absence, one of the ways of limiting competition and reaping the benefits of monopoly.

Because the land market can undermine the goals of governments the flow of influence ought to receive attention from political scientists as well as economists. History is full of examples. When the British government decided to abolish the local property tax on agricultural land in 1929, the declared objective was the provision of help for struggling farmers at a time of recession. This purpose was defeated by the landowner, who exacted higher rents from his tenants. The exaction was possible because the increase in the farmers' disposable income was not offset by a rise in the costs of production; so the money from the tax cut was a surplus which could be transformed into rent.

The same thing happened with the tax relief granted to families buying their homes with the aid of mortgages. The intention of public policy is the encouragement of home ownership. Politicians believe that the purchase of a house is more readily within the reach of a family that can offset part of the cost of the mortgage against income tax liabilities. (In Britain, that tax concession costs the Exchequer £5bn per annum.) But the logic of this proposition is dubious. The tax benefit has long been capitalised into higher residential land prices. This means that the value of the tax relief, having helped to raise the price of housing land, has damaged the prospects for newcomers who want to buy homes.

Why do the advocates of new policies fail to take account of the rent effect? The most charitable explanation is that the social and economic costs of distortions are concealed by the deficiency in the data on the land market. This is well illustrated by the way in which city governments in the USA attempt to encourage renewal of their central districts by attracting developers with offers of substantial 'holidays' from their property tax liabilities. Magnificent edifices have been constructed as a result of this inducement, but no account is taken of the wider consequences. The expectations of the owners of neighbouring vacant sites are elevated at least as high as the nearest gleaming skyscraper. They realise that they can capitalise the saving in property taxes into higher prices for their land. The result, not intended by the policy-makers, is that it becomes even more difficult for entrepreneurs and families to remain in the cities, and the displacement of the population to the suburbs continues apace. A similar economic effect was experienced in Britain when the Thatcher government granted exemption from rates, the local property tax, within areas designated as Enterprize Zones: rents rose to neutralise the benefit that was supposed to go to the prospective users of the land. This undermined the main objective of the tax relief, which was to create more jobs in pockets of high unemployment in the cities.

What are the lessons stemming from this discussion? One is that costly mistakes would be avoided if policies could be scrutinized for their effect on the use and value of land. If this information were available, the distortions would be fewer, and the valuation process itself would be simpler.

Under the present system, in which government influence over the market skews the distribution of income, we cannot be sure where the dividing line is between economic rent (the surplus after the costs of labour and capital have been met in a competitive economy), and what might be termed political rent (that portion of the income that would otherwise have gone to entrepreneurs and/or employees if governments did not distort the distribution of income). The market place, which is neutral, today records the income going to land as 'rent'; but we can see that a free and efficient market in land would chronicle a somewhat different value, probably to the advantage of wages and profits.

Another lesson has major implications for the general belief that governments help people and firms by giving them money or special dispensations. We have seen how the benefits of special tax treatment are hijacked by the owners of land, with undesirable consequences. By taking into account the theory of rent, we realise that many more goals would be achieved if a means were found for blocking the propensity of landowners to sidetrack the taxpayers' money which was aimed at helping others. A satisfactory solution would have the effect of reducing the level of rents, or slowing up their rate of increase.

International Trade

The case for assembling an accurate inventory of the stock and value of a nation's natural resources is not limited to domestic considerations or even purely economic ones. This study does emphasise arguments built around the need to optimise the returns from the ownership and use of real estate.[6] But there are wider sociological and political reasons for monitoring the trends in the land market which transgress the boundaries of sovereign nations. The price of land in one country has a fundamental impact on the livelihoods of people on the other side of the world, and can even affect international relations. This hypothesis is illuminated by the case of Japan.

In 1988, the value of Japanese land was worth more than the land in the USA, Canada and France combined (Table 1:I). Population density does not provide a complete explanation, for central Tokyo is less densely populated than Manhattan or Paris. Given the paucity of data on rents and the land markets of North America and of Europe (with the exception of Denmark: see Chapter 11), one could be forgiven for imagining that this difference in values did not matter; that a close scrutiny of rental trends in Japan would yield little of significance to the factory workers of Birmingham, Alabama, or Birmingham, England, compared with, say, the relative costs of labour which are the subject of much rumination in orthodox analyses of the balance of foreign trade. Our proposition is that the price of land is crucial. We can consider this by

Costing the Earth

Table 1 : I
Real estate in four countries

	Japan	United States	France[1]	Canada
Area (km²)	377,800	9,363,500	549,000	9,976,000
Density (person/km²)	324.7	25.5	100.8	3.0
Value of land[2]	4,540.0	2,950.0	172.1	256.2
(per cent GDP)	317.5	74.7	29.4[3]	70.1
(per cent wealth)	54.9	21.0	7.6[3]	19.9
Value of housing				
(per cent GDP)	49.7	88.4	153.9[3]	64.0
(per cent wealth)	8.6	24.9	39.8[3]	18.2
Value of non-residential structures				
(per cent GDP)	48.9	50.0	92.8[3]	140.0
(per cent wealth)	8.5	14.1	24 [3]	39.8

1 1983.
2 Dollar billions at purchasing power parity exchange rates in 1985 (which value a dollar at Y 222, FF 7.27 and C$ 1.22).
3 The value of structures includes the value of underlying land.

Source: OECD 1988:75, Table 24, and references therein.

examining the housing sector and tracing the impact of the cost of the roof over the heads of a family living in Chiyodaku to the lifestyles of a family on Long Island or the Isle of Dogs in London's East End.

In Japan, the exceptionally high price of land is directly responsible for the extremely poor quality of housing. Accommodation compares very unfavourably with standards achieved in other market economies. Should we care about the price of urban land in Minatoku or Setagayaku, and the way in which the very low property tax leads to the under-utilisation of urban land? This issue has been considered by the Organisation for Economic Co-operation and Development (OECD), whose economists concluded that a higher tax on land values was the appropriate remedy.

The international implications may ... be significant. Lower land prices would reduce the size of the down-payment needed to acquire a house, and this might reduce savings and encourage greater investment in housing. By thus affecting domestic saving-investment balances, this change would tend to reduce the current external (trade) surplus (OECD 1988: 78)

In other words, the price of land is a severe constraint on the lifestyles of the average Japanese family. It shapes the economic behaviour of men and women who squeeze on to the bullet trains every day to endure the long commuting trip to the Sanyo or Nissan factories. It forces families to save more than they would otherwise wish to, if they want to buy their houses one day. This produces very high rates of capital investment and comparatively low domestic demand, which compels Japanese manufacturers to seek their markets in other countries.

All of this translates into a significant impact on the consumption habits and employment prospects of citizens in the countries to which Japan exports her products. It has been known to squeeze out firms in North America and Europe which would otherwise be producing goods for their local consumers, and it creates political friction and the demand for limits to free trade.

The knock-on effects of the land market, then, are evidently fundamental. Yet the Secretaries of State who periodically convene to try and solve the economic problems generated by unbalanced international trade *never* discuss the price of land. The prices of borrowed money and of hired labour are scrutinized in minuscule detail. The land market, to judge by the silence, might just as well not exist.

Some Current Issues

A finer appreciation of the nature and value of rent as a stream of income emerges if we explore some contemporary problems and the way in which they might be resolved.

The efficient use of resources. Despite two centuries of scientific and technological progress, and the perfection of the systems of mass production, millions of people suffer from inadequate incomes and homelessness. Many of the problems stem not from the fact that natural resources are finite, but from their wasteful use. That waste arises not through over-exploitation — the focus of anger of the political 'greens' — but through under-employment. The scale of that waste is disguised by the failure both to measure the value of land and to understand the allocative processes. A particularly poignant example will serve as an illustration.

The rich industrial nations throw away fortunes because they allow those who control land to misallocate valuable sites. The rot begins in the central city areas. Instead of using urban land in an optimum way, some owners choose to hoard their sites and allow them to stand vacant, or they limit the sites to some temporary under-use such as car lots or seedy porn shops. The motive of the owner is rational: by not placing the site at the disposal of potential users today, larger capital gains will be made tomorrow. The owner cannot be blamed for acting in his best interests; the responsibility for permitting this state of affairs rests with the community.

As a result of this speculative behaviour, people are displaced to the urban periphery or deep into the countryside. What happens? *Per capita* incomes are reduced, as some people are compelled to live and work on land that is not so well endowed as the tracts from which they, or their parents, were displaced. The cost to the population does not stop there, however, for now governments are obliged to increase the tax burden to finance the extra roads, sewers, hospitals and other amenities that the new, far-flung settlements require to make life tolerable. As new schools and community centres on the social periphery are erected, at great capital cost, local governments board up schools and community centres in the hearts of their cities for want of people to use them!

Geographers and demographers study this pattern of displacement. The process could be equally well monitored by economists if they had at their disposal maps which tracked the changes in land values. It would then be possible to compute the value of the capital that was being wasted, which would open up the prospect of an informed debate. The alternative ways of spending these resources could be explored, with the aim of enhancing the quality of life based on a more vibrant pattern of land use and population distribution. For the present, we have to rely on the informed view of one of the leading land economists, Professor Mason Gaffney of the University of California (Riverside):

The high marginal cost of adding to spreading cities, and the low true value of the additions, are concealed, in our culture, by an elaborate and pervasive system of subsidies and cross-subsidies built into our institutions, and political power structures, which act to drain the old centres to feed the fringes. In a systemwide accounting we find the true social cost of urban sprawl as we know it today to exceed the gains at the margins. We are not so much adding land to cities as wasting capital (Gaffney 1986 : 15).

The Tax Burden   The call for a reduction in the taxes that fall on people who produce the wealth of the nation was favourably received by politicians in the 1980s. The demand for lower tax rates, however, was not associated with an appreciation of how governments could reduce spending obligations to avoid running up a massive Reagan-style budgetary deficit.[7] The net result was that there was no reduction in revenue requirements; the same amount of money had to be raised from somewhere, and the extra burden generally fell on people receiving low incomes.

Real estate is very lightly taxed and could generate a greater proportion of public revenue. How much could be raised by a tax on property? And should that tax fall on the profits of capital (the buildings on the land) or should it be directed exclusively at the rent of land? Some answers are suggested by the levy of Value Added Tax on non-domestic construction in Britain as from April 1989.

This tax challenges the government's strategy of encouraging renewal of the fabric of the inner cities. A tax on capital improvements raises the cost of production and occupation and undermines the aspiration of an urban renaissance. An inevitable consequence is that fewer jobs will be provided in the pockets of high unemployment, and the vicious circle of population displacement will continue at an accelerated rate.

What would happen if the revenue was raised exclusively from the rental value of land? The answer depends on when and how the tax is levied. In the case of the Value Added Tax, it is payable at the point when the owner surrenders his interest in the land. This has an important economic consequence. The selling price of land is correspondingly reduced, for the net income that prospective owners can now expect is reduced. This, however, provides owners with an incentive to postpone the sale of their land. This version of a tax on land, then, is double-edged. A lower price is good, in that it opens up fresh opportunities for prospective users. But because this is not in the landowner's interest, he is likely to withhold his sites from use as long as he can. The holding costs associated with a vacant site are zero in countries such as Britain, which do not impose a property tax on land that is not being used, or insignificant, as in the United States, where the tax rate is set at a very low level or the assessed values are seriously out of date. And the rental income that is foregone today is more than recouped through the sale — at much higher prices — tomorrow.

VAT on land, then, repeats the errors that were made by successive Labour governments in Britain. For philosophical reasons they wanted to capture part of the community-created land value, but the taxes and levies which they selected were poorly structured and were ultimately abolished.

The nature of rent is such, however, that an efficient land tax can be constructed that would achieve the desired objectives. It would have to be levied at a uniform rate and fall on the annual rental value of land. Such a tax is the most neutral (and therefore the most efficient) of all fiscal instruments. This is not a controversial claim. Today's economists corroborate the findings of the classical economists to the effect that the tax on economic rent does not induce distortions or generate any loss in welfare. It is, in the words of Milton Friedman, 'the least bad tax' of the lot (Harrison 1983: 299). The tax cannot be shifted forward on to prices (Samuelson and Nordhaus 1985: 402), which means that the economy is not placed at a competitive disadvantage in international trade, as it is by other taxes. And it is perfectly neutral with respect to the allocation of resources (Lipsey 1979: 370), which means that it enables the market to operate efficiently.

Why, then, has it not been adopted by governments which are concerned to free people to maximise their incomes? The full answer has to be sought in the history of the struggle over property rights and the evolution of the democratic process (Douglas 1976). Even without these considerations, however, it is not surprising that politicians are reluctant to enter into an exploration of a policy without first knowing how much the tax could raise: hence the need for a valuation of natural resources.

The Tax Base In reforming the structure of taxation, governments have to take account of the buoyancy of the tax base. Natural resources represent a vast source of as yet untapped revenue. The radio spectrum is an example of a source of exploitable revenue, the full value of which has yet to be measured.[8]

Resource rents provide an ever-expanding base for taxation because they grow effortlessly in step with every improvement in the living and working conditions of a community. This underlying process is disguised because governments tend to make decisions about their spending programmes without analysing the full impact on rents and without attempting to directly capture even a part of that revenue for the public purse. One result is that less efficient taxes are preserved, which limits enterprise. Additionally, the decision-making process on public investment projects may be distorted, which can lead to missed opportunities. A project that is otherwise socially and economically necessary may be rejected because of the apparent, rather than the actual, balance of costs and benefits. Yet far from being financially unsound, the project may enhance the value of neighbouring land to the point where, coupled with user fees, the increased rental revenue could be sufficient to underwrite the cost of the investment. The controversy over the financing of the railway track connecting London with the Channel tunnel on the Kent coast is instructive.

On March 8, 1989, British Rail announced that it would run one-third of the 68-mile track through tunnels, adding another £500m to the cost. The decision was not based on the rational assessment that the investment would meet the 7% profit criterion set by the government, but as a result of public outcry against the blight on the value of some residential properties along the route and the threat to the rural environment. The initial reaction from City financiers (reported in *The Financial Times* on March 10, 1989) was that preserving the environment for the residents of Kent seriously weakened the commercial viability of the project. The government did not disabuse the financiers; it merely warned that the money would not come from the Exchequer. The Prime Minister told the

House of Commons on March 9 that it was 'government policy that users of the new line should pay the full cost, rather than the generality of taxpayers,' since they were the ones who would enjoy the benefit of the railway.

In fact, others were also going to reap some of the economic benefits from the presence of a high-speed link between the capital and Kent. These benefits were precisely measured by the increase in the value of land. Residential land in the commuter areas around the Medway towns and the coastline between Dover and Folkestone rose in anticipation of the improved transport link with central London (indeed, the benefits extended right into France: property values along the French coast rose in 1988 because these attractive rural areas were now going to be within daily commuting distance of the City of London). The benefits were also capitalised into the rapid rise in commercial, industrial and recreational land around Ashford, the town designated to operate as a link on the new Chunnel line.[9]

From a social cost-benefit analysis point of view, there may be no tension between the financial and environmental goals associated with the selected railway route and the construction plans. To test this, however, analysts would have to take into account the upward movement in land values as well as the decrease in prices of some real estate near the track. Nor need the financing considerations have been perceived as a problem. For if the owners of land whose assets increased in value were required to contribute towards the cost of the undertaking which bestowed its benefits on them, the financial outlook for the project would have been transformed. The cost burden could have been spread more equitably among all the beneficiaries of this improvement in the system of mass transportation.

The Privatisation Programme A feature of the post-Keynesian era is the desire to reduce the scale of public sector involvement in the wealth-creating process. Governments, it is contended, cannot better the performance of the individual in a market economy that is free and efficient. One way to alter the balance in favour of private enterprise, according to the advocates of the supply-side theory, is by selling publicly-owned real estate. This runs down the level of public involvement in economic activity. Margaret Thatcher led the way with this strategy, which in the late 1980s raked in £5bn a year. Her success was much admired and emulated by President Ronald Reagan and endorsed by the Bush Administration.

The efficacy of this strategy from the standpoints of either economics or ethics is not a subject to which we shall address ourselves here. The point we wish to highlight is that the public purse was deprived of many millions of pounds because of the valuation procedures employed in the privatisation of real estate. Critics were able to point out that land sold to the private sector was then resold for many more times the price which the public coffers had received, thereby apparently depriving the taxpayer of a great deal of revenue that might have been used to finance the health service. In fact, the government faced dilemmas which could not be properly resolved without having at its disposal the land value tax.

The use to which land can be put is constantly changing: recycling it is the one countervailing force against the fact that its supply, in aggregate physical terms, is immutably fixed by nature. When real estate is sold, it is not always possible to anticipate alternative higher-value uses to which it could be put: the needs of the community sometimes shift at a very rapid rate. At some stage, however, the seller has to place a price on the land which reflects the current market realities, and strike a deal with a buyer.

But does this mean that the government has to write off the large increases which might accrue to the new owner once, say, new housing needs of the community are expressed in the rezoning of industrial land for residential purposes? Not if the government is taxing the rental value of land. As soon as values increase, because of changes in user demand and planning permission, the Exchequer immediately recovers a part of that enhanced value. So while the direction of future changes in values cannot be anticipated, in perpetuity, for the purpose of agreeing on a selling price, the increase (or decrease) in land values can be accommodated into perpetuity by the land value tax.

Had this fiscal policy been at the disposal of the Thatcher government, some serious political embarrassments — and fiscal losses — would have been avoided. Take, as an example, the decision to privatise the 10 water boards. The prospect of the transfer of their 500,000 acres to private investors caused considerable political opposition to the government's plan. The Thames authority, in particular, owned vast tracts of land in the London area which, in a drained state, would yield a fortune in rental revenue. But the valuation of the assets, at the time of disposal, cannot take into account the value that would accrue on the hypothetical possibility that the choice sites would one day receive planning permission for a more valuable use. Valuation is based on current opportunities available to prospective users.

The suspicion persisted, however, that in private hands, some of the land would be drained and developed for commercial and residential use. We can now see that this added value need not be lost to the community if the increase in rental values produced additional revenue for the Exchequer through the tax on rental income.[10]

The Future of Mankind

The lessons derived from the British case study (Part 2) can be generalised in global terms, and indeed the justification for a programme of further research can be mostly readily discerned from the stark ecological implications of *not* gathering more information about land. Valuation exercises will have to be conducted for every country in the world if the appropriate policies for husbanding the resources of nature are to be framed. Encouragingly, the world's statesmen appear to be unanimous in promising that they will confront the ecological issues during the 1990s. The prospects for defining sound remedies are not good, however, for there is an insufficient awareness of the origins of the crises.

Over 40 years ago David Bidney (1947:571-2) warned that economics, among the other social sciences, 'may reach a stage of incoherency which renders [it] unsuitable as a guide to consistent policy and conduct,' leading to a cultural crisis which he defined as 'the direct result of some disfunction inherent in the very form and dynamics of a given form of culture' (1946:537). On the evidence before us today, it seems that this stage has now been reached. The creation of the 'hole' in the ozone layer, the destruction of the Amazon basin, the deforestation on the slopes of the Himalayas which regularly floods the Indian sub-continent and kills people by the thousand, are just a few of the dramatic cases of systemic behaviour that is inconsistent with the preservation of man's ecological niche. The conceptual framework employed by economists, and on which politicians rely, fails convincingly to identify the roots of the problems.

Environmental and social crises, which are inter-related, are not inevitable. The responsibility for them rests not so much with economics, as a scientific discipline, as with the use to which it is put (or not put) by its practitioners. The steadfast refusal to plumb the depths of the land market is evidence of this, yet there are no remedies for the ecocrises that do not include a heightened awareness of the value of economic rent and the processes of the land market. The world does not have the time for prevarication or the trial and error approach — of learning lessons the hard way. An example may concentrate our minds on the relevant issues.

The Bush Administration's initiative on the Third World foreign debt, which in 1989 topped $1.3 trillion, stemmed in part from concern about the political impact of the greenhouse effect. Changes in world temperature by up to five degrees centigrade in the next 50 years are predicted to shift the balance of economic power between the Have and Have-not nations, and between the capitalist and socialist blocs. Political stability is essential during this period of ecological uncertainty. According to senior US officials in Washington the situation in Latin America is grave enough to warrant writing off part of their foreign debt. But who would benefit? The unemployed inhabitants of the *favelas* of Venezuela? Over 300 of them died in riots while protesting against the economic 'reforms' that were deemed necessary to fund the $38 bn debt. Would debt 'forgiveness' help the landless peasants of Mexico (debt: $108 bn in 1987) who, in desperation, have resorted to squatting on other people's farms in the hope of making a living?

Cancelling part of the debt amounts to the infusion of billions of dollars into these less developed countries (LDCs) which, under the existing tenure and tax regimes, would benefit the price of land rather than provide work for the landless. (A similar economic effect was produced in countries such as Colombia by the inflow of billions of dollars from the narcotics trade.) It would reinforce the distribution of income and asset values in favour of landowners, and would not encourage LDC governments to restructure their economies in favour of efficient markets. The implications of the rent effect ought to be weighed in the balance when we search for solutions, for what might be intended as an altruistic rescue operation by the Western banking system could serve to aggravate the structural defects in the economies of the LDCs. This becomes clear as we identify the links between economics, politics and ecology.

The major dynamic behind the over-exploitation of parts of the environment is the process by which hundreds of millions of people are displaced onto marginal land by the tax-and-tenure systems. In desperation they over-work resources that ought to be carefully nurtured. For every careless corporation plundering the resources of the Third World for a quick profit, before moving on to fresh opportunities, there is a legion of penniless peasants whose time horizons have been truncated by the need to search for the next meal. They are the ones who, like locusts, are forced to scorch the earth for sustenance, the inter-generational imperatives of their cultural heritage long ago destroyed by the intrusions from without.

Now, what are the consequences of raising the attractions of land as an investment medium by writing off part of the foreign debt? The West would reward the motives that played a large part in the under-use of those tracts that ought to be put to full use, the best acres in and near the towns from which the highest incomes could be generated, those very acres from which the landless have been expelled or from which they are denied access.

Being forced to repay the debt, on the other hand, need not be an economically painful process for those LDCs that neutralized the rent effect. If the pricing mechanism was made to work properly, the debt repayments flowing out of the country would be matched by an implosion in the land market: the burden would work its way through the system and ultimately fall on the *rentiers*. Instead of there being a deleterious impact on the capacity to produce wealth or raise living standards, the reduction of rental levels would lead to full employment and a rise in wages as the resources available to the economy were put to efficient use.

There would be a political price. Such a strategy would provoke hostility from the elites who control the LDCs. They are already on record as warning that the West should not interfere with their sovereign rights, which includes the right to determine the manner in which they exploit their natural resources. The sovereignty argument does not address some important questions that are fundamental to global survival. For example, who owns the oxygen produced by the Brazilian rainforests? Earth's ecological system works as a symbiotic whole: nature does not recognise territorial boundaries.

Diplomacy of the highest order will be necessary if these politically sensitive issues are to be properly debated, but it has to be admitted that the quality of analysis and advice offered by Western governments and scientists to LDCs does not invite confidence. The jet-set consultants as a class are perceived as not particularly well tuned into an appreciation of the nature of the problems that underlie the spill-over onto marginal lands. The manner in which Brazil (debt: $124 bn. in 1987) is censured for building the trans-Amazon highway is a case in point. What is the purpose of Western condemnation if no account is taken of the reasons why landless people from the fertile, under-used areas of the southern provinces migrate to the relatively inhospitable Amazon basin in search of a livelihood? Without such an appreciation the 'strings' attached to such help as is proffered usually only serve to intensify, rather than mitigate, the economic pain.

But there is no mystery as to the origins of the problems. A World Bank economist, Hans Binswanger, has already exposed the political character of the Brazilian ecological crisis. Fiscal and monetary policies encourage the extensive acquisition and hoarding of land, which triggers a leapfrogging chain of events. Businessmen buy farmland to reap the tax benefits, which then encourages the farmers to proceed to the Amazon where they stake their claim to tracts of land to qualify for favourable tax benefits! The owners of land in Brazil, then, both inside and outside the Amazon, are not so much farming the land as farming the Brazilian taxpayer. The tragic result is that fertile land in the south is under-used while fragile land in the Amazon basin is over-exploited.

One of the anomalies identified by Binswanger (1988) is the senseless structure of the tax on land. This is levied on unimproved land but is reduced by up to 90% on land used for crops or pasture. Forests are classified as unimproved land and therefore taxed at the full rate, which induces settlers to chop down the trees to reduce their tax liability. None of this would occur if the tax was an *ad valorem* one on the current realisable market value and was levied irrespective of how the land was actually used.

The need for a balanced solution to the Brazilian land market is emphasised by the Association of Researchers of the National Institute of Amazon Research (Inpa), which — as part of the strategy for saving the rainforests — advocates agrarian reform and an end to land speculation (reported by Louise Byrne in *The Observer*, London, March 12, 1989). The removal of damaging fiscal incentives and the implementation of a properly-constructed tax on the market value of land would lead to the optimum utilisation of the best farmland and the preservation of the ecologically vital (but economically poor — in terms of modern farming methods) lands of the Amazon. These concrete measures would stem the flow of people northwards. Wages would rise and the demands on the public purse would diminish, which in turn would enable the government to operate a prudent monetary policy. The temptation to inflate the currency, which is a favourite trick to disguise the structural imperfections and tensions in the economy, would also diminish. If the value of money is stabilized, another benefit to resource conservation accrues: the propensity to buy and hoard land as the best hedge against inflation is eliminated.[11]

Political controversy is unavoidably associated with any radical strategy involving questions of property rights and taxation policies. Creditor nations prefer to avoid such delicate issues, which go to the heart of every power structure. But if effective remedial action is to be instituted, they will have to be addressed. Only then will it be possible to define sustainable alternatives to the social institutions and economic processes that are encouraging man to debase mother Earth.

NOTES

1 Letter from Bill Robinson dated Nov. 7, 1983, to Henry Law, referring to Bill Robinson and Geoffrey Dicks, 'Employment and Business Costs', *Economic Outlook* (October 1983:18-25).

2 We assume a 9% rise in earnings in 1989 and 1990. This is a worst-case position, for the government, but a best case assumption from the viewpoint of people financing mortgages. The rapid escalation of wages and salaries in the mid-1970s saved many homeowners from defaulting on their mortgage commitments; the land speculation of 1970-73 stretched household budgets to breaking point, and the same thing happened between 1986-89.

Table 1 : II
Income as percentage of UK National Income

	Urban rents (GB)[1]	Income from employment and self-employment (UK)[2]
1985	13.6	83.9
1986	14.8	85.1
1987	16.8	83.8
1988	21.2	82.3
1989	24.5	83.0
1990	26.5	85.0

1 Disaggregated from Table 2:II.
2 *UK National Accounts*, London: HMSO, 1988, p.13, Table 1.3. Our estimates for 1988-1990.

NOTE: The national income as calculated in the UK accounts includes rental income received by home-owners, which is an imputed value, but understates the rental value of land because

(i)   it excludes the rental income that ought to be imputed to land in other categories, in both the public and private sectors, which are not yielding a cash income; and

(ii) the valuation measures current use values, which in many cases are lower than if all sites were efficiently employed (as expressed by the needs of users in the market) within the guidelines set by the planning system.

This explains why the two columns in the table may add up to more than 100%, even excluding profits (not all of which would be included as profits in a properly constructed total of national income, for the official statistics misleadingly incorporate into this category land rent received from owner-occupied trading property).

Our estimates in Col. 1 only cover revenue that could be realised in the marketplace. They therefore exclude, for example, 115,000 hectares of urban land deemed to be undevelopable (see Ch. 8 and footnote to Appendix 1). This land is excluded from the data on urban area that was used as the basis for our calculations of total land values (Table 4 : VII).

3   The boom in the UK housing market that originated in the South-East in 1985 caused the escalation in the cost of mortgages which turned into a matter of death on December 12, 1988. During the two preceding months, British Rail electrician Brian Hemingway was obliged to work every weekend, and extra hours of overtime throughout the week, to finance his £250-a-month mortgage. He accepted responsibility for faulty workmanship in the signalling system that led to the crash of a train bound for Waterloo in which 35 passengers died.

4   Economists, despite their proclaimed dedication to positivism, have failed to employ some of their key terms in a scientifically consistent way. 'Rent' is the most abused. A recent example is by Nobel Laureate James M. Buchanan, who uses the term 'rent seekers' to classify those people who seek to manipulate the political process to their pecuniary advantage. See his 'Post-Reagan Political Economy', in *Reaganomics and After* (London: IEA, 1989, pp. 2 and 10). Americans have a perfectly adequate term for the activity of manipulating money out of the public purse: they call it the politics of the pig trough. There seems no good analytical or taxonomic reason why rent, given its classical association with land, should be diluted in this manner. For a systematic analysis of the history of the misuse of the concept, sometimes under the guise of evolving economic theory, see Gaffney (1982).

5   Soviet economists, who now have to reacquaint themselves with the theory of markets and the pricing mechanism, have yet to grasp this point. Gorbachev's principal economic adviser, Abel Aganbegyan, thinks that 'for historical reasons the prices for natural resources and agricultural products have been depressed, since these did not include rents ... (Aganbegyan 1988 : 133). The price of an item of food does *not* include an element of rent, payable for the use of land. This was clearly articulated by the classical economists, but it still needs to be reaffirmed.

6   Advocates of free market economics usually restrict their censures to governments which fail to uphold the appropriate standards of stewardship towards assets in the public domain. Surprisingly, however, even private owners display a cavalier attitude towards their real estate. Many companies in Britain have only the 'sketchiest notion of what they owned or occupied,' declared David Yorke, President of the Royal Institution of

Chartered Surveyors, in a speech to a CBI conference in London on January 24, 1989. But there is an expectation of improvement. 'The major change we are now seeing is the growing acceptance of the need for a property strategy and of the fact that this cannot begin without a clear, constantly updated, inventory of property holdings.'

7   For the United States, this dilemma was documented by Stockman (1987). In Britain, the problem was solved by a programme of public sector disinvestment. This contributed to a £14 bn budget surplus in 1989 but left many services (notably, the roads and mass transit systems) seriously under-financed. One economist concluded: 'If Britain were spending as high a proportion of GDP on public-sector investment today as the Heath and Wilson governments our £14 billion budget surplus would be wiped out. The extent of the government's neglect would be revealed if an annual statement of the worth of the public sector's assets and liabilities had to be produced' (Brian Reading, 'Budget ignores value of our public assets', *The Sunday Times*, March 12, 1989).

8   The Thatcher government proposal to market the airwaves over Britain by auctioning commercial TV franchises was not popularly received by existing franchise holders, the 16 commercial TV companies whose profits were estimated to have been £265m (1988). They argued that competitive tendering — more precisely, bidding a rent — for the privilege of using the airwaves would result in a deterioration in the quality of programmes. They claimed that what they regarded as the comparatively poorer quality of broadcasting in the USA was the fate that would befall British viewers. This is a curious contention, because American TV companies do not pay the full economic rent for the privilege of using a scarce resource.

Two British companies, Thames and LWT, explored a dodge to see if they could stay in business without paying the UK government a full market rent. Between them they paid £43m in 1988 for the licences to broadcast in the London area. Renting satellite time and beaming their programmes from outer space would cost them £2m (*The Guardian*, March 18, 1989). This ruse reveals the need for the world community to agree upon a united approach to renting outer space to commercial users in the same way that the Law of the Sea has stimulated a debate, through the United Nations, about the need to charge a rent for the use of the oceans. The rental revenue could be expended on globally useful projects.

9   The announcement of the extra building costs for the railway raised the value of shares in construction companies. Blue Circle, the manufacturer of cement, 'scored a double gain as investors re-evaluated its land bank in Kent,' reported *The Observer* on March 12, 1989.

10   The way in which the land value tax option provides a solution that encompasses environmental and economic considerations is illustrated by

the history of a 63-acre site occupied by Delhi Cloth Mills. In 1962 the city's administration ordered the closure of the textile factory on pollution grounds — then reversed its decision and opposed the closure because the owners would make large windfall gains if the site was used for commercial and residential purposes. The matter was resolved at the end of a 5-year legal battle when the Supreme Court ruled in favour of the company. This judgment was forecast to speed up the redevelopment of valuable industrial sites in the major cities throughout the sub-continent (David Housego, 'City Centres in India likely to be redeveloped', *The Financial Times*, London, March 29, 1989). If the Delhi authorities had spent as much time and effort in adopting the appropriate property tax — the one that fell on land values — it need not have worried about the prospect of windfall gains going into private pockets. It could have secured a cleaner environment for the citizens of Delhi and clawed back part of the enhanced rental value that was created by the community in the first place.

11   Ecological and economic problems rooted in the tax-and-tenure structure are not peculiarly associated with the Third World, it must be stressed. Alabama, the US state which proudly calls itself 'the timber basket of the whole world,' illustrates the hypothesis that there is a high correlation between the distribution of land and the displacement of population. A county-by-county analysis revealed that the greater the concentration of ownership, the higher the rate of out-migration and the lower the rate of economic growth.

This study, significantly, was not an official one (three-quarters of Alabama's senators own land other than the sites beneath their houses), but was sponsored by a newspaper. See *The Birmingham News*, February 5 and March 4-6, 1989. Some politicians and university scholars are quoted as blaming the property tax. Alabama's rates are the lowest in the USA, which does not encourage landowners 'to make their holdings more financially productive.' Owners can legally demand to be taxed on a 'current use' basis: so by planting timber they pay a minuscule tax of less than $1 an acre on assessed values that are a fraction of the free market prices that prospective users would be willing to pay for land — if they could get it.

PART TWO

2

Terra Incognita

RONALD BANKS

DISPUTES over rights to real estate have caused the most vexed problems throughout the ages. Controversies have been variously resolved by civil commotion and military conflict; at other times, consensus has emerged around new theories of political philosophy. The final word about these rights has not yet been carved on tablets of stone: they continue to be redefined by parliaments, civil courts and social conventions. It is one of the greatest ironies, however, that while people argue (and nations fight) over 'Who owns what?', very little attention is directed at the problem of 'What's it worth?'

Government statisticians and university economists devote a great deal of care to collecting information about labour and capital, but they generally show little interest in the scarcest of productive factors — land. We know precisely how many workers there are in the market economies of the world, and have a fair idea of the value of the wealth that they produce. We have measures of the size and value of the capital stock, and detailed records of who owns it and how much they earn from it. But when we turn to land, we are confronted with a dearth of data. This is particularly notable in the United States, where the information-collecting agencies are otherwise exhaustive in their efforts.

In Britain, the Domesday Book of Norman conquest times was the first thoroughgoing nationwide appraisal of the value of real estate. Since then, apart from the survey commissioned by Lord Derby in 1874, little of value about the ownership and value of land (beyond the estates controlled by the aristocracy) has been produced in which we can have confidence. This was the problem that challenged the authors of this study.

The value of land — that is, the value separated from that which must be attributed to undepreciated capital improvements (buildings, roads, drainage systems and the like) — does not receive systematic attention from economists or the civil servants who are the keepers of the nation's books. This does little to enhance the quality of the decisions taken by the politicians who are entrusted with the task of maximising social welfare.

An explanation for this seemingly contemptuous indifference towards land might be found in the view held by eminent university teachers of economics that the rental value of land constitutes a small proportion of the nation's income. Professor Paul Samuelson (1976: 538) guessed that economic rent was 'probably' only about 5% of GNP. Professor Richard Lipsey (1979: 371), in discussing the revenue that might be reaped from a tax on economic rent, contended that it 'would finance only a tiny portion of government expenditures'. Graham Hallett (1979: 88), an authority on the economics of European real estate, has expressed the view that the rental value of land 'can hardly be more than 2% of national income'. These views reflect the opinions of past masters such as Joseph Schumpeter, who — in reviewing the argument that the rent of land constituted a substantial tax base, a view originally expounded by the French physiocrats — asserted that this 'involves an unwarranted optimism concerning the yield of such a tax' (1954: 865). The uniform view that the rent of land is a relatively insignificant value has been associated with an equally startling absence of facts upon which to base the assessment.

The hypothesis that rental income is a negligible fraction of the total revenue of a nation was regarded as testable by the authors of this enquiry. Britain was selected as a case study. The methodology employed is fully reported in the hope that scholars in other countries will conduct similar exercises.

The guesstimates of the authorities cited above were found to be grossly out of line with reality, as can be seen from Table 2 : I. The capital value of land in Britain, in 1985, was about £505 billion. Using the interest rates appropriate for that year, and including mineral rents, we arrive at an annual rental value of over £53 billion. To that figure must be added that proportion of income from the rates (Britain's local property tax) which constitute land rents; the market price of land, which we measure, is net of this tax liability. The yield from rates in Britain totalled £13.37 billion. If we assume that the rental value component constituted 35% of this total (our calculation of the national average ratio of plot prices to house prices), we must add £4.7 billion to our estimate to get near a true figure of rental income (£58.2 bn).

This was equivalent to 22% of national income. Viewed another way, rental income, received or imputed, but not counting rates or mineral rents, exceeded the income tax paid by people. That the sum involved is far from the derisory quantity suggested by economists is rendered clear by the fact that all the rental income of Britain in 1985 was equivalent to 44% of all central and local government tax revenue, including National Insurance Contributions.

These valuations have been criticised as *under-estimates* by

Table 2 : I
The value of land in Britain, 1985

	Capital value	Rental value	
	------- £ billions -------		% rate
In public services	64.4	3.2	5
Farm, wood and forest land	48.3	2.4	5
Housing	249.0	19.9	8
Commerce	107.7	8.6	8
Industry	35.5	4.4	12.5
	505.0	38.6	7.6*
Mineral rents/royalties		14.9	
Local authority rates		4.7	
TOTAL	505.0	58.2	

NOTE: numbers do not add up due to rounding.
* Implicit

experts in the landed professions and property development business to whom they were submitted for scrutiny. We accept this criticism. Owing to the shortcomings in the data, some working assumptions had to be made. As a matter of policy, the authors chose assumptions that would yield conservative estimates.

The buoyancy of income from land can be gauged from the trends in rental income in the last half of the 1980s (Table 2 : II). We estimate that the rental income in 1988 was £86 bn. Our calculation takes into account the weakening of agricultural rents since 1985, and the decline in North Sea oil rent. These losses, however, were more than offset by the dramatic rise in urban land prices, beginning first with residential site values and followed, late in 1987, by the accelerated increase in the price of commercial and industrial land. We estimate the rental income of land in 1990 at about £119 bn.

Table 2 : II
Estimated rental value of land,
Britain: 1985-1990 (£ billion)

	(1)* Land rent	(2) National income	(3) Land rent as a % of national income
1985	58.2	260.3	22.4
1986	55.2	276.5	20.0
1987	66.2	303.3	21.8
1988	85.7	336.7	25.5
1989	104.6	363.6	28.8
1990	118.8	387.3	30.7

* Includes imputed rents and 35% of local authority rates. Explanatory data are in footnote 1.

Without adequate data on rental income we do not believe that the economists who advise governments can offer credible guidance on the macro-economic consequences of the alternative strategies that are available for achieving social and economic goals. We need a detailed appreciation of the size of the flow of income from land, to present an accurate assessment of the impact of various policy options that might be directed at, say, regional or inner city regeneration, or fiscal policy. As things stand, however, decisions are taken in almost total ignorance of — because of lack of interest in — the impact of the land market, and the consequential effects on people and businesses.

We recognise that, as advisers in the realm of practical affairs, economists start from a point of disadvantage. They have allowed theory to degenerate to the point where it is now difficult to disaggregate their data, so it becomes difficult to know where — in value terms — natural resources (land) end, and man-made equipment (capital) begins. Despite the difficulties, however, it is important that the hiatus in our knowledge should be filled.

The Spatial Methodology

We used the spatial method of assessment: of multiplying areas of land by the price per hectare that the sites would command, given the various uses to which they could be put under the system of planning now in place in Britain. This is the direct route into the problem, and is recognisable as an extension of the use of what is known as the comparative method (the assessment of value in the light of known prices realised for similar sites).

We double-checked our approach by applying the residual method of assessment to commercial and industrial land, the sector in the property market with the least reliable data on the amount and value of land used. This method consists of an assessment of the capital value of a completed development reduced by the costs of the developments on the land and an allowance for the developer's risk and profit. As a first step, this entailed the multiplication of the floorspace areas of buildings by rental values (Chapter 8). This method has been employed by national accounts statisticians at the CSO, although with strong reservations (Bryant 1987 : 100).

Our method produced the higher capital value (£143 bn, compared with an estimate of £135 bn achieved by applying the residual method). The two methods routinely produce different results, but in the real world there are practical ways of resolving such anomalies. As a report by the Department of the Environment noted:

> The residual method is commonly used by developer-purchasers and the comparative method by landowner-vendors, though both parties may use both methods as cross-checks on each other. More often than not the two methods give different results and the outcome will be a negotiated price whose level depends on the relative negotiating strength of the parties ... (DoE 1988:18).

The comparability of the two values which we achieved gives us confidence both in our approach and our estimates for the other sectors.

The significance of our findings suggests the need for an official assessment of the rental income of the nation. Which method ought to be used? Our spatial method would be favoured, if only by default. For the residual method cannot now be applied at the regional and national levels. The Department of the Environment has discontinued collating floorspace statistics, a decision criticised by two of the major firms of property surveyors, Hillier Parker and Healey & Baker (Chorley 1987:187).

Portfolio Management

An awareness that Britain has wasted part of her precious natural resources has emerged in recent years. Conservative governments have appealed for better use of these resources as part of a strategy to restructure both the economy and taxation.

To clarify the issues and understand why the problem arose in the first place — so that appropriate corrective policies can be formulated — a closer examination of the dynamic differences between the land and capital markets ought to be sponsored by government and the institutions with a direct interest in the property market. For land and capital markets display some uniquely dissimilar characteristics. The consequences of the motives which influence decision-making are also strikingly different, and have major implications for policy.

The work in this field has been limited. Yet the importance of understanding the land market is evident from the continuous pressure on local authorities and State agencies to sell assets that have been surplus to their requirements. Although the political emphasis has been on the better use of publicly-owned assets, an improved use of privately-owned real estate would also raise living standards: a University of Cambridge study found that one-third of vacant land in England's cities is owned by the private sector (DoE 1988 : 35).

Unfortunately, a comprehensive inventory of the nation's stock of natural resources is not available. This gap in our knowledge has been identified time and again. The public, for example, are kept in ignorance of the full extent of property owned by local authorities. This was the conclusion of the Audit Commission (1988 : 1), which characterised property as 'a hidden and undermanaged resource'. The value of local authority property was guessed to be over £100bn., excluding council housing. Is it satisfactory that we should have to guess at the value of property administered in the public domain? How can councillors be held accountable for the way in which they manage property if the electorate cannot judge the efficiency of that management in balance sheet terms?

> There is nearly always an opportunity cost associated with holding property. But this cost is frequently ignored in local government decision-making. It is not uncommon for development proposals to be perceived to be cheaper than they would otherwise be 'because we already own the land'. Authorities should be aware of the alternative land use values of their property and this awareness should be communicated to all those responsible for taking decisions concerning property. Equally, users should be aware of the opportunity cost of using property inefficiently in terms of excess running costs. (Audit Commission 1988 : 12)

In the public domain, then, it would seem — according to the Audit Commission's investigation — that the taxpayer would benefit enormously from a systematic programme of identifying and valuing landed property. The benefits would be measured in terms of untying capital resources that are not fully used; generating capital receipts; cutting the tax burden; and encouraging a dynamic economy. The money involved is not inconsiderable. The Department of Health and Social Security have estimated that annual revenue savings from making better use of their estate may range from between £300m and £500m (National Audit Office 1988a : 4).

> Yet few authorities recognise [their holdings] as investment property
> and manage it accordingly, e.g. by valuing it in order to determine the
> rate of return being achieved. The value of this property can be very
> great ... Without knowing the value of the investment portfolio it is
> impossible to measure the return being achieved. (Audit Commission
> 1988:17)

The Land Register, which is supposed to be a compilation of vacant
sites available for redeployment to new uses, is evidently an unsatis-
factory record both as an inventory of land and as a tool for
implementing policy. The Audit Commission discovered that it
lacked credibility as a source of information to potential developers.

> Not many authorities know how much vacant property they own. The
> Register of Unused Land on which authorities are required to register
> their holdings, does not record all vacant property, e.g. if it is being used
> for some temporary and sub-optimal purpose such as surface car
> parking or grazing. Few authorities have procedures for periodically
> reviewing their vacant land holding and justifying its retention. (*Ibid.*)

According to a detailed survey of vacant urban land (Civic Trust
1988), over 60% of unused land and small sites were not recorded
on the register, because most of them were in private ownership.

Parts of the private sector can be as negligent as the public sector
in failing to record their assets in terms of current market values.
The difference, of course, where such assets are owned by public
companies, is the prospect of action by ever-alert predatory entrepreneurs. They seek companies at knock-down prices (the direct
result of under-valuation of properties) for the purpose of stripping
them of their assets.[2]

It should be acknowledged that the valuation of property at
current market prices is not universally accepted as a necessary
precondition for judging the efficiency of people who are charged
with managing assets. This was the view expressed in 1982 by the
Commissioners who administer the Crown Estate, the capital of
which belongs to the Sovereign. The Crown Estate had until then
never been comprehensively valued.[3] The Commissioners, when
questioned by the House of Commons Committee of Public
Accounts, argued that the absence of a full valuation did not
necessarily compromise their performance.

We pressed the Commissioners on whether the absence of a balance sheet recording all their assets and liabilities made it difficult for Parliament or any interested outsider to form any assessment of their efficiency of operation of the Crown Estate, and whether a proper return was being obtained from the capital expenditure being incurred. The Commissioners expressed some doubts whether formal valuation of their assets would provide a sound tool for measurement of the efficiency of their management (Committee of Public Accounts 1982:vi-vii).[4]

There is merit in the argument that, in some circumstances, non-financial considerations should override the decisions that would otherwise be taken on the basis of the pursuit of the greatest profit. Protecting the environment, for example, is in certain circumstances a good reason for putting conservation before pecuniary gain.[5] But that is not a justification for not placing a price on the natural heritage, and disclosing that value in the books for all to see. In an open, democratic society, informed decisions can only be taken when the fullest possible information on the 'opportunity costs' — the alternative benefits — of one decision or policy, as against another, are monitored and understood.

It is towards a better understanding of issues such as these that we present this study.

NOTES

1   The national income for 1985, 1986 and 1987 is taken from the Blue Book for 1988. We subtracted 2% for Northern Ireland — approximately its proportion of the UK's GDP at factor cost in 1985 (*Regional Trends*, 1987:123). Growth at current prices of 11% is assumed for 1988, 8% for 1989, and 6.5% for 1990.

Local authority rates income for 1985 and 1986 is taken from *Social Trends* (1987:113:1988:111) with a small deduction for Northern Ireland. It is assumed to increase in line with national income thereafter.

The estimated land rent of Britain for 1985 is given in Table 2:I. The figures for later years have been calculated after taking into account the rental trends in each of the major sectors:

(1) Agriculture. The *Property Market Reports* indicate that farm rents may not have increased during 1986 and 1987. Thereafter it is assumed that as farmland prices begin to pick up rents increase roughly in line with inflation, say 5% per annum. The Ministry of Agriculture, Fisheries and Foods' weighted price index for vacant possession sales in England rose by

one-third in four months from a ten-year low applying roughly to the spring of 1987.

(2) Minerals. The economic rent of the North Sea oil and gas fields is assumed to have fallen by 60% in 1986 and to have stabilised in 1987 in line with the government's tax and royalty income. This drop accounts for virtually the whole of the decline of rent's share of national income in 1986 (col. 3). Thereafter it is assumed to decline by a further 33% in 1988 as prices weaken and output falls, and then stabilize. No account has been taken of trends in other mineral rents.

(3) Urban land. Urban land rents are believed to have doubled between mid-1985 and mid-1988, for the following reasons.

The Halifax House Price Index rose by 59% from June 1985 to June 1988 and the housing stock probably grew by 2.7% over the same period, raising the total market value of GB housing (including tenants' interest) from about £685bn (implied by the official balance sheet figures — see Chapter 6 and *Regional Trends* 1988 : 61) to £1,119bn. Using this study's estimate of the value of the land under houses, the buildings alone were worth £445bn in 1985. *Building* magazine's House Building Cost Index rose by 17.3% over the next three years, Coupled with the 2.7% stock expansion and a notional 3% improvement in the quality of the average product, this raises their value to £552bn. By subtraction, the value of the land under houses in 1988 was £567bn, 136% higher than in 1985 and half the value of the housing stock as opposed to 35% in 1985.

We are dealing here with capital values. Rental values would not have increased as much if yields were falling, which they may well have been in the speculative boom. If we assume they fell from 8% to 7%, then residential land rents would only have doubled during the period.

In the commercial and industrial sectors we may deal directly with rental values. Commercial and industrial rents were slower to start accelerating than house prices, but the former did so in 1987, and the latter followed in 1988. According to the Summer 1988 issue of Healey & Baker's *PRIME* report, prime retail rents rose by 66% between June 1985 and June 1988, prime office rents by 57%, and prime industrial rents by 55%. RICS' General Building Cost Index rose by about 15% during the same period. If we make the same assumptions about stock and quality growth as in the residential sector, and assume that land rents were 40% of land and building rents in 1985, then land rents rose by 125% to £29.3bn in 1988, when they reached 55% of land and building rents.

We conclude that urban land rents at least doubled in the three years after 1985. We assumed a decelerating rate of increase for 1989 and 1990, because of the impact on residential land prices of the government's interest rate policy. But this did not convert the land market into one that favoured buyers, for builders continue to be 'dogged by the fundamental

problem of inadequate supply of land for housing to meet ... demand'
(House-Builders Federation State of Trade Enquiry, Feb. 1989). This
ruled out the prospect of an early weakening in residential land prices.
Taking into account the partial deregulation of the tenanted sector of the
housing market, we estimate annual rates of increase from 1985 as follows:
15%, 25%, 40%, 25% and 15%.

The total for each year in Table 1 :II, column 1, is the sum of the market
rents that would be obtainable from all sites in Britain if they were being
used to full economic potential within existing planning constraints. As
these rents do not always reflect the existing use of sites, or the actual rents
paid or imputable, they are not comparable with the national income.
They would be comparable only if all sites were used in an optimal way.
Likewise, the capital values associated with these rents (Table 2 : I) are not
comparable with the capital values in the national balance sheets.

2   Britain's brewers, the owners of a vast estate of prime-site properties,
have until recently failed properly to measure the performance of their
assets in terms of rental income. One of the biggest, Courage, decided in
1988 to alter its arrangements, giving shareholders a better perception of
how their assets were being used. According to David Brierley, writing in
The Sunday Times on May 15, 1988: 'Courage's scheme is basically a
balance sheet operation which forces the brewer to pay an "open market"
rent for the pub to [a] property company. "Paying a market rent will
certainly concentrate our minds," says Michael Foster, the managing
director.'

3   The Commissioners, as trustees, manage 250,000 acres of agricultural
land, urban properties which are concentrated in central London, and
mineral rights on land and under the sea. Their view at that time can be
contrasted with that of the National Audit Office (1988 : 2, 12), which
argued that 'the absence of a reliable data base is a serious impediment to
rationalisation', without which 'there is a danger that surplus land and
buildings will be retained or that disposal of the wrong sites will take place'.

4   The Commissioners altered their approach in 1984, when they
undertook a comprehensive valuation of the Estate. Within four years, a
new system of annual valuations was adopted, which resulted in a
significant realisation of asset values. Valuable land that had been locked
away in a 'land bank' has been developed, and in 1988 the Estate was valued
at about £1.4bn. A new system of portfolio analysis was instituted with the
aid of a computer data base, which assisted the Commissioners to
undertake a significant diversification of the assets at their disposal. This
analysis is now regarded as a major tool for portfolio management. (For a
critical appreciation of the new approach, see National Audit Office
1988b.)

5   It remains to be proved that there is a necessary conflict between sound

Costing the Earth

ecological practices and the free market. The evidence in the main demonstrates that it is monopoly power — exercised within the context of an imperfect market — which permits people to abuse natural resources. The injurious practices of agriculture, for example, are the direct result of State protection. A free market would sponsor sound techniques that relied less on extensive farming methods and the intensive exploitation of chemicals; both these latter approaches to food growing damage the land and the social milieu of the countryside, and are the direct result of Common Agricultural Policy subsidies which enable farmers to sidestep the disciplines of the pricing mechanism and the requirements of consumers (Body 1987).

3

The Nation's Balance Sheet

ALEX HARDIE

POLITICAL philosophers have traditionally supposed that the main purpose of the (minimal) State is to protect property, chiefly landed property, and that property rights could not exist in the absence of the State (e.g. Hobbes 1651). It is not surprising therefore that a number of philosophers as far back as the French Physiocrats and the classical English and Scottish economists concluded that the rent of land is a peculiarly suitable source of revenue for financing the primary duties of the State — defence of the realm, administration of the law and maintenance of social order.

It comes as a particular surprise, therefore, to discover that the State makes no effort accurately to ascertain the location, area, or value of the land titles which it is protecting, and is thus denied the opportunity to charge directly for the service which it is rendering. In this it compares poorly with insurance companies, which have an analogous economic role. An insurance company compiles a complete inventory of all the houses and other property that it insures, both as to stock and value.

This anomalous situation is of comparatively recent origin. Historically, the main fiscal burden of the State fell upon landowners. This was true in the Anglo-Saxon period, and also during the feudal period. The privilege of landholding carried with it the duty of serving the ruler in war, or providing a cash payment in lieu of service, and maintaining law and order at the local level. It was only after the feudal period that the cost of financing the primary duties of the State was shifted onto other forms of income.

Economists and philosophers can offer sound arguments, based on considerations of both efficiency and equity, why the fiscal obligation ought to be returned to the direct beneficiaries of the security offered by the State. However, if the government is to accomplish this, it must have a full inventory of all land at its disposal. This would present few difficulties, for land is easy to identify, value and tax (in contrast to the taxation of personal property which is easy to conceal).

The State does now provide an occasional inventory of property in the UK, in the form of national balance sheets (Bryant 1987). However, these figures are not complete. Both tangible assets (sub-soil deposits such as coal, gas and oil, historic monuments, works of art and antiques) and intangible non-financial assets (patents, copyrights and trademarks) are excluded, on the grounds that they would be too difficult to value.

Nor do they provide a break-down of real property between land and what were traditionally known as 'improvements' to land, i.e. buildings and structures. Some use is made of existing data on site values, but no effort is made to value sites separately, even though this is advised in the United Nations recommendations for national balance sheets (Bryant 1987 : 109).

Land values are incorporated in the official estimates for buildings plus sites. If these are valued correctly it should be possible to derive land values as a residual by deducting the values for buildings alone, using separate Central Statistical Office (CSO) estimates for the UK capital stock. A weak estimate of UK land value is made by this method in a supplementary note, but it is not included in the official statistics (Bryant 1987 : 100; for the results, see Chapters 6 and 8 below).

Valuing land as a residual leads to problems. The capital value figures will be wrong if the life of buildings is wrongly estimated. Also a decision must be made whether to value structures at gross or at replacement cost. The latter is appropriate for commercial buildings, but the former may be more suitable in the residential sector, where older dwellings tend to be worth about as much as new dwellings. Architecture, materials, character, accommodation, and garden size may all be superior in old buildings, which would tend to offset depreciation. Though all buildings need repairs, prudent homeowners in effect make good depreciation as it occurs and thus maintain the value of buildings.

For the public sector, the lack of market valuations for many buildings and works makes it difficult to reach sensible figures for land values. 'Low and sometimes negative' estimates (depending on the year) are obtained for local authority residential buildings, 'from which it would appear that the cost of construction ... is not reflected in the values which these buildings might fetch on the open market' (Bryant 1987:101). This situation is predictable given that the buildings are erected for subsidised letting to those who cannot afford open market housing, that they are erected in estates which tend to depress the value of individual houses, and that the whole effect of this is registered in individual site values.

However, the valuations were based on valuations made during 1983/4 in connection with sales under council tenants' Right To Buy legislation, adjusted roughly to compensate for the likelihood that the dwellings sold under-represented high rise flats and estates where houses are difficult to let (Bryant 1987:112). Anecdotal evidence of the higher than average capital gains in store for buyers suggests that Right To Buy valuations tend to be under-valuations, perhaps because the effect of the gradual privatisation of estates itself is not taken into account.

As for public buildings and works, there are no market values for these assets because they are not traded at all, and an assortment of ways of calculating their depreciated current replacement costs has to be found. Whereas central government has made some attempt to value its real estate (see Chapter 9), very few local authorities have done so. Local authorities are required to produce figures for flows, not stocks. Thus their investment each year in real assets is known, but the value of their real estate is not. According to Bryant, the official view has been that finding out the latter for each local authority would be expensive and not worthwhile, as it would not lead to policy changes. Central government's only concern is the amount of debt they owe, and in Bryant's opinion there is no correlation between assets held and debt accumulated (Hardie 1987; for a valuation based on debt, see Chapter 9).

In the private sector, market values clearly represent less of a problem. For residential buildings the aggregates are calculated from rateable values up-dated and converted to capital values using the 5% sample survey (20,000 dwellings) of building society mortgages conducted by the Department of the Environment (DoE). The value of tenants' rights is ascertained by taking the vacant possession value of dwellings and deducting local Valuation Offices' estimates of landlords' interests. (The same fraction of vacant possession values is assumed to apply in the local authority sector.)

The same methodology is applied to commercial and industrial properties, up-dating and converting rateable values to capital values with the aid of a specially commissioned sample survey undertaken by the Inland Revenue Valuation Office in 1985 (see Chapter 8 and Appendix 1) and the Investment Property Databank's price indices. For the break-down of these properties between the sectors of ownership (personal, commercial and industrial companies, banking, other financial institutions, public corporations, and central and local government) current cost accounts are used where possible with rough adjustments to take account of intervals between balance sheet revaluations. However, the correct but laborious approach of sampling company accounts is not undertaken in the commercial and industrial sector. Instead the value of the real estate of these companies is taken as the residual after the value of such assets in all other sectors has been calculated. Though 'reasonable results' are claimed (Bryant 1987:115), this claim seems optimistic.

Other real estate, belonging to charities, universities, social clubs, sports clubs, etc., is also valued using rateable values and 'limited evidence of modern rental values and rough capital valuations'. Sectorisation of these assets is particularly 'broad brush' (Bryant 1987:114-116).

Rough estimates are made of the value of local authorities' unused land. House building sites and land with planning permission for residential development are valued using the DoE's estimates of the average value of such land, but data is scanty on land banks held by builders. Sites with permission for commercial development plus construction sites are valued at 2% of the value of buildings (Bryant 1987:112, 114, 116). This proportion is taken directly from Jack Revell's original work on the national balance sheets in the 1960s and no attempt is made to obtain a more realistic estimate (Hardie 1987).

Omissions of items which contain land value, in addition to minerals and historic monuments mentioned above, suggest themselves: these include vacant and derelict land in the private sector, airwaves, street parking, moorings, foreshore and beaches, reclaimable land such as the Wash, fisheries, sea and estuaries.

The National Income Accounts

An alternative approach to calculating the land value of the nation might be to deduce it from the National Income Accounts. Unfortunately, these offer little scope for evaluating land rent. They give figures for rent, but not figures for rent on land alone, and even the overall rent figures exclude certain elements of rent. For example, while there are estimates of imputed rent for owner-occupied houses, rent is not imputed for any other owner-occupied property. The existing use rents of owner-occupied trading properties are implicitly included in the gross trading incomes of the industries concerned, but the rents of owner-occupied non-residential non-trading properties are not included in the national income at all (CSO 1985: 248).

In the National Income Accounts there is only one entry which relates to transactions in land and existing property. This shows the transaction costs involved when these assets are bought and sold. However, these costs are not closely correlated with the values of the assets.

Need for Improved Land Value Statistics

Political Duty   The public sector has an enormous portfolio of real assets. For efficient financial management it should review its portfolio. In the absence of a routine assessment, it is not possible to monitor performance in a satisfactory manner. Central and local government are not profit-making bodies but they must pay interest on their debt so they cannot ignore return on investment. They hold assets on behalf of citizens. If asset management is inefficient, citizens who pay taxes suffer by having to carry a higher burden than would otherwise be necessary.

Public corporations have a target rate of return, and the concept applies to the rest of the public sector; the principle of opportunity cost holds here as elsewhere. Sensible guidelines should be established for new investment. Portfolio review may reveal some assets that are no longer needed, and others that yield little return. Assets that are held by government but are no longer needed tie up funds which could be used to finance new investment. They are also withheld from the private sector, which might make profitable use of them. Assets yielding little in their current use could be redeployed to better uses.

There is one particular asset which is often under-used, or entirely unused, when owned by the public sector — land. Local authorities and public corporations own vast tracts of vacant and derelict land. If the government seeks to manage the economy it certainly ought to start by making the best possible use of its own resources. If it does not set a good example, its exhortations to citizens to be more efficient cannot carry weight.

We often hear that land is a valuable asset, especially as a riposte to suggestions that public sector bodies should sell some of their holdings. But a valuable asset is one that yields a high return. To calculate return it is necessary to know the flow of income from an asset, putting a cash figure to income obtained in kind, such as free office accommodation or training areas for the army. It is also necessary to have a market value for the asset. Yet estimates for income obtained from land are either inadequate or altogether lacking. The government does not even know how much land the public sector owns. Most local authorities do not know the size of their landholdings, and their assets are normally valued at the price at which they were acquired, perhaps many years ago. Therefore, the public sector cannot say whether the yield on its land is high, low or zero.

The government spends £17 billion on debt interest each year. If it could sell off land that it no longer needs and thus cut down its borrowing requirement this would help to reduce the cost of servicing the debt. Citizens ought to have a figure for the imputed rent of government owner-occupied property, for it is an implicit tax which at present they pay without knowing its amount.

Macroeconomic Policy   Even nominally 'non-interventionist' governments claim that they have an important role to play in increasing employment, controlling inflation, balancing international trade, reducing cyclical movements in the economy and encouraging faster economic growth. Various policy instruments are used: the public sector's own income and expenditure decisions, the central bank's activities, direct intervention in markets, advice to companies, and exhortation to citizens to change their economic behaviour.

To be effective, macroeconomic decision-making requires accurate and comprehensive statistics. Governments have at their disposal a plethora of data on national income, expenditure and product; government income and expenditure; imports and exports, financial flows, price changes, and so on. Information on stocks as well as flows is needed, and indeed we have figures for the labour force, the national debt, the amount of notes and coins in issue, and the total assets and liabilities of financial institutions. However, though there are figures for rent, but not for rent of land alone, successive governments have been content to be ignorant of the value of the nation's land, the value of the land used by the various sectors, including themselves, and the value of the land not used at all.

Common sense would suggest that unemployed land leads to unemployed people. Yet discussions of 'unemployed resources' never include unemployed land. We hear that the labour market is imperfect, but we never hear about the imperfections of the land market. The conventional macroeconomic view is that unemployed land indicates a lack of demand. If this were true land prices would fall drastically during periods of high unemployment. If there was lower demand for land for building houses, offices, factories and shops, the price of land would drop, the supply of land being the same as before. But land prices do not necessarily fall, which shows that the land market is very different from, say, a commodity market.

The fact that land is also a marketable asset affects prices. The supply of land does not in fact stay the same as before — landowners can hoard it in the expectation that conditions will improve. Commodities have to be stored, unemployed people have to be supported, and unused machinery has to be maintained, but land can be kept out of use without imposing any maintenance costs. Vacant land, however squalid or dangerous, can be left alone without prejudicing its value for agriculture or construction. The owner who makes no use of his land is entitled to prevent anyone else from using it, and receives full legal protection for his property rights, even though he pays nothing to the State in return.

Given that land is a necessary input for every human activity, and that the land market is imperfect, a government that is serious about unemployment should take action to bring unused land back into use. The first step would be to ascertain how much unused and under-used land there is in the country, and to whom it belongs.

Discrete Data for a Discrete Resource　Land is a factor of production but is qualitatively different from capital. Land is the gift of nature; it is not created by human thought and effort. It is restricted in amount; no more can be created. It is a marketable asset which keeps its value and typically appreciates over time. In contrast, 'capital', referring to buildings, vehicles, plant and equipment, is often non-marketable and certainly does not keep its value — it depreciates rapidly or becomes obsolete. But more can be created at any time. Conversely, 'capital', referring to money and financial assets, is not a factor of production — it is a collection of marketable assets. Again, more can be created at any time.

Land and productive capital are part of the nation's wealth; money and financial assets are not, except where they represent a claim on the rest of the world. Financial claims within a country net out. The idea that land is 'really' just a form of capital is therefore wrong: land is unique in being both a factor of production and a highly marketable asset. Investors understand the difference. They speculate in land, as in commodities, financial assets and currencies. They do not speculate in machinery or oil refineries. Land is the only productive asset which is subject to speculation.

As we have seen, the asset role of land can interfere with its role as a factor of production. No owner would deliberately keep a factory out of use. If land was also purely a factor of production every owner of land would keep it in use all of the time, for even a low rent would be better than none. But land is a marketable asset which may actually offer greater long term returns to its owner (though not to society) if it is kept out of use at the present time. When prices are low, holding sites out of use may help raise prices. When prices are rising rapidly, sites may again be held out of use in expectation of yet higher prices, which will help fulfil those expectations. Thus land tends to be artificially short in supply and its price artificially high.

In Latin American countries land is kept out of use even though landless peasants would be keen to use it. In densely populated Britain most of the Scottish Highlands is deliberately kept out of farming use, and there may be over 1m hectares of land which is derelict and waste (Moss 1981:142). Even in London, where a hectare of land can sell for millions of pounds, there are thousands of hectares of vacant sites. Schemes to restore such land run into the obstacle that the owners will often not sell except at unaffordably high prices (Civic Trust 1988:31).

Microeconomic Policy   Academics writing about land often put forward arguments which could be true only if the land market was close to perfect. Yet of all asset markets the land market exhibits the most imperfections.

The asset is not homogeneous. Recall the adage about buying property: 'Location is everything'. One house may have a fine view of the sea, the next house no view at all. Thus there are natural monopoly aspects to land. There are man-made restrictions as well. Substantial amounts of land are held by a few owners, who can affect the price. Transaction costs are high, with legal fees, stamp duty, payments to estate agents and auctioneers, and also to the Land Registry. Fraud is easy. The potential buyer's knowledge is often poor: there is no market place, merely a series of deals. Prices fetched are usually kept secret, apart from properties sold at auction. A new owner can conceal his identity.

Insider knowledge is invaluable for making profits from land dealings. Having influence with officials or councillors can also help. The planning system adds greatly to imperfections in the land market, and in some cases has led to bribery and corruption. Rent controls affect the value of both built-up property and farmland.

The land 'market' is important, and advocates of free markets must aim to improve their operation. Better information is a prerequisite for an efficient land market.

Fiscal Policy   We began by noting the philosophical tradition that, logically, property owners ought to pay for the minimal State. The introduction of a significant measure of land value taxation would both meet this requirement and tackle directly the conflicts arising from the dual nature of land. Such a policy implies a comprehensive valuation of the nation's natural resources.

A National Cadastral Survey

'Cadaster' is a word of Latin origin, and cadasters were well known in the Roman Empire. A cadastral survey would be perfectly feasible in the UK. It would show for each plot of land its exact location and dimensions, with correct boundaries, its present and permitted uses, its value as estimated at a particular date as recent as possible, and its current owner. It could build upon the statistics already available in the Land Register. Revaluation would take place at regular intervals.

The law should be reformed so that an entry in the Land Register would be proof of ownership. The Land Registry fee could be higher than it is now, and the profits could be used to finance the survey. (Even now the Land Registry makes a profit.) The National Cadastral Survey would be open to inspection by anyone, and landowners would be entitled to query the values attached to their land. Those accustomed to the cumbersome English system of secret conveyancing and expensive legal fees may be surprised to learn that land registers are common in other parts of the world, such as Australia. Jersey, in the Channel Islands, has always had a land register system, and nineteenth century reformers considered that Jersey's prosperity could be attributed to its small proprietors, whose existence was due to the legal simplicity of purchasing land (Arnold 1880 : 302-303).

A national cadastral survey would provide comprehensive figures for the value of the nation's land as a whole and of its regions, and for the value of the land owned by the various sectors of the economy, or devoted to particular uses. The British Government has not considered undertaking such a survey in modern times. Even the national and sector balance sheets, which are excellent in many respects, do not have an assured future. According to the statistician in charge of these accounts:

> Further updates of tangible asset values will be made when resources permit and depending on the contribution it is considered they can make to government assessments of economic developments. From a statistical viewpoint more regular updates would undoubtedly yield benefits in the quality of valuations possible because methods would be continually reviewed and improved (Bryant 1987:101).

Regrettably, there are no current plans to compile complete balance sheets after the 1987 estimates in the 1988 edition of the CSO Blue Book.

4

Urban Land

DAVID RICHARDS

ATTEMPTING to discover the amount and composition of urbanised land in Britain is rather like grappling with the plot of a complex whodunit: witnesses have observed events at different times, in different places, for different reasons, and with varying degrees of attention, and one problem is to establish why their accounts contradict each other.

Sophisticated land use monitoring systems, such as Tyne and Wear's Joint Information System, exist only at the local authority level, and even where they do exist it has generally not been thought to be cost-effective to map the results and analyse the maps. This is despite the clearly recognised need to assess the effects of the national land use planning system which has been in operation for over 40 years (Fordham 1975: 71, 83; Rhind and Hudson 1980: 16; Dickinson and Shaw 1982: 343).

To calculate the areas of the urban land uses of Britain in the mid-1980s we therefore have to consult an assortment of mainly out-of-date surveys, conducted for special purposes, using various methods with varying degrees of accuracy, and producing results which are not directly comparable.

Sources of Evidence

A national spatial referencing system has been created in Sweden, and has been called for by the Chorley Report for the UK (Chorley 1987). The National Land Use Classification was produced by government departments in 1975, but has found little application. The Department of the Environment's Joint Circular 71/74 to all local authorities in 1974 requested annual returns on land use change classified into the fifteen major orders of the NLUC. Peter Walls, the DoE's Principal Research Officer, however, noted that 'response rates were never sufficient for any one year to provide a comprehensive national or regional picture and the requirement to provide them was dropped in 1979' (Walls 1984: 27).

The DoE turned to the data collected by the Ordnance Survey during the course of its normal map revision process, and in January 1985 began a three (now extended to four) year trial implementation of a system developed by Roger Tyme and Partners (DoE 1986 and 1987). This monitors change in 24 mainly urban categories, and it was intended that two other DoE initiatives would produce results compatible with its new classification. One is a feasibility study, by the same firm, of possible sources and methodologies for a regular national land use stock survey. This remains as yet unpublished, awaiting clarification of the Government's view of the planning system. The other, in conjunction with the Countryside Commission, is a project to develop a method for monitoring landscape change (Hunting SC Ltd 1986), which has produced land use stock information, but mainly for rural areas.

The DoE's only project to date to measure the stock of specifically urban land uses has been the Developed Areas survey of England and Wales, which used air photographs taken in 1969 (DoE 1978). Peter Walls wrote that 'the technique used was not thought worth repeating when air cover was made available by the RAF for 1980/81.' The DoE therefore relies mainly on Dr Robin Best's, and his successor Dr Margaret Anderson's, analysis of transfer of farmland to a very broad 'urban' category recorded in the annual June Agricultural Census (eg. Best and Anderson 1984).

Best's only research on the components of urban land use, and its total stock as opposed to incremental change, applies to 1951 and 1961. He used the local authority Development Plans of the early 1950s and the improved Town Maps of the early 1960s, in conjunction with demographic data, as his source materials. He multiplied the mean urban land provision per person for a 'representative' sample of settlements within each of several settlement categories by the aggregate census population of that category to obtain the total urban area (Best 1981: 59). For its decomposition into the various urban land use categories, he was limited to the rough classification employed by the local authorities. As for up-dating, he was thwarted by the Town and Country Planning Act of 1968, which made town maps 'an extinct species'.

Two other privately initiated surveys of the nation's land use were consulted for this study. The Second Land Utilisation Survey of England and Wales, inspired by Sir Dudley Stamp's pre-war survey, was directed by Dr Alice Coleman in the 1960s. During the decade some 3,000 volunteers, many of them school children, recorded their field observations on 6,500 six inch Ordnance Survey maps. A further five man years work was involved in sampling 151,000 points on the maps to produce area measurements. Five per cent of the area was then re-surveyed in the 1970s. By 1977, however, only 15% of the coverage had been printed, and in 1979 the Government announced that it would not be completing the job as the classification was 'unsuitable' and the information out-of-date (Rhind and Hudson 1980: 65). Dr Coleman has since become involved in other areas of research, and much data remains locked in computer files.

In 1974 Richard Fordham published estimates of the urban area of the UK and its regions. He systematically point sampled a sample survey of Ordnance Survey maps. It was found to be necessary to sample 124,000 points to produce an estimate of the UK total for which there was a two-thirds chance that it was accurate to within 5% (Fordham 1974: 48). His classification of land uses within urban areas was limited by the information contained in topographical maps, and as fewer observations were obviously recorded for each of the three main sub-divisions than for the urban area as a whole their accuracy was lower — there was a two-thirds chance of the true figure for each lying within 20% of the estimate (Fordham 1975: 76). Fordham saw his emphasis on the need to determine the degree of accuracy of estimates as one of the main contributions of his study, 'on the principle of the devil you know.' With Best's and Coleman's methods the degree of accuracy cannot really be known, but the accuracy of their raw data is bound to be much less than that of the OS topographical maps.

Other estimates of the urban area of England and Wales exist. Tony Champion (1974) used a technique similar to Best's to produce almost identical results. Margaret Anderson (1977) and

Guy Swinnerton (1974) independently point sampled Ministry of Agriculture land classification maps and again produced similar results. These are set out, as given by Best, in Table 4:I, but with one adjustment: Best noted that Champion assumed a two-thirds larger area of land for isolated dwellings, and this extra 90,000 hectares has been subtracted from Champion's total.

Table 4 : I
The urban area of England and Wales in the early 1960s, according to four surveys

	Effective date	*Urban area ('000 ha)*	*% of total area*
Anderson	1962	1,460	9.7
Best	1961	1,490	9.9
Champion	1960	1,466*	9.7
Swinnerton	1962 (?)	1,480	9.8

* See text
Source: Best 1981:44, 63.

The Urban Aggregate — England and Wales, 1961

Best concluded (1981: 77) that 'there is now fairly general agreement that the urban area of England and Wales extended to approximately 10% of the whole land surface in 1961.' In making this statement he had in mind also the surveys by Coleman, Fordham and the DoE (Developed Areas), but to assess its truth we shall have to look into the matter of urban definition, and the problems of comparing different classifications of urban land use. The results of this investigation are set out in Table 4:II.

Each of the surveys in Table 4:I used virtually the same definition of urban land, one determined by the Ministry of Housing and Local Government in its *Report for 1958*. According to Best,

urban land may be defined as the built-up area with its associated open spaces and transport land. In more detail it comprises the so-called four main urban uses ... of housing ['net residential area' — the aggregate plot area of dwellings (including gardens) plus any small associated open spaces and service roads and paths], industry, open space and education, together with the 'residual urban uses' which are listed as 'railway land, waterways, principal business and shopping use and public buildings, together (where applicable) with mineral workings, derelict land, airfields, government establishments, land used by statutory undertakings and miscellaneous uses'. In practice, most opencast mineral workings and military land, in the country as a whole, fall outside the bounds of measured urban land ... It should also be noted that farmsteads, along with other isolated dwellings and development [transport] in the countryside, are recorded as urban land (Best 1981: 29, 59).

The classification of reservoirs was not clear (see Best 1981: 121). It was decided that these probably were not included as developments in the countryside, and that their extent in developed areas was not worth considering.

Fordham suggested that his own definition 'differs only in that he [Best] included some special non-urban uses and this survey excludes public parks' [and cemeteries and allotments] ... 'because no means of identification from the maps existed' (Fordham 1974: 30-31). He also pointed out (p. 5) the impreciseness of Best's categories: 'the four major land uses were defined in Development Plans as being "primarily" in the given use.'

We can only guess at the amount of open space not included by Fordham, and the amount of mineral workings and derelict land included by Best. Coleman gives the most detailed breakdown of urban land, and it is assumed that her figure for 'open space — sport' (82,000 ha) covers Fordham's 'formal recreation land', and that the rest of her open space (95,000 ha), plus allotments (32,000 ha), represents the extent of his omissions. It is also assumed that 10,000 ha each of mineral and derelict land were measured by Best. These areas are added to Fordham's estimates, as is Best's figure for civil airports.

Fordham's major sub-divisions of urban land are unique in that he included the gardens of houses as open space rather than residential land. However, this anomaly may be ironed out by subtracting the assumed figure for 'formal recreation land' above from his 'open land' estimate. This leaves 383,000 ha for gardens, which has been added to 'buildings' to give, with mineral/derelict land, the figure in Table 4 : II.

All the findings quoted from the Second Land Utilisation Survey, taken from a list supplied by the Survey, have been adjusted to exclude the 43,000 ha recorded by Best (1981: 88) for urban growth from 1961/62 to 1963/64 (the median date of the Survey). This growth has been distributed proportionately between all the land use categories. The Survey's *Field Mapping Manual* (Coleman and Shaw 1980) shows that the 'settlement supercategory' includes all mineral workings, derelict land, and airfields (ie. military, too), and excludes allotments. All but 34,000 ha of the former have therefore been subtracted, and the latter have been added in Table 4 : II.

Upon the Developed Areas survey Best registered the following verdict:

> The definition of the urban area as a whole, though not of its component land uses, coincided fairly closely with the one used here, except that mineral workings were wholly included . . . . [Due to the small scale of the aerial photography] it was only possible to map and measure continuous areas of developed land of 5 ha and above. As a result, small developed sites and part of the transport system were not included in the calculations, whereas conversely, some agricultural and rural land was improperly absorbed because of the generalising of boundaries (Best 1981: 64).

The 1:50,000 scale of the maps, and the reliance of photo interpretation on ground cover features, meant that the functional classification was limited to five vague categories, three of which — residential, industrial/commercial, educational/community, etc. — begin with the adjective 'predominantly' (shades of Best's 'primarily'). The other two were transport and open space. On the plus side, however, is the fact that the coverage was exhaustive and the boundaries were digitised for computer processing, avoiding the inaccuracies of sampling (DoE 1978: 1).

In Table 4 : II the following assumptions have been made: the mineral land of the Hunting survey (below) was the measured extent of such land outside 'urban' areas in 1969 — so 30,000 ha has to be taken out (from the industrial category); 10,000 ha was all the derelict land measured (that not surrounded by developed land was ignored, as were reservoirs not adjoining developed areas — DoE

Table 4 : II

Five estimates of the urban area of England and Wales in 1961, harmonised to Best's definition of 'urban' and divided into common land use classes (in '000 ha).[1]

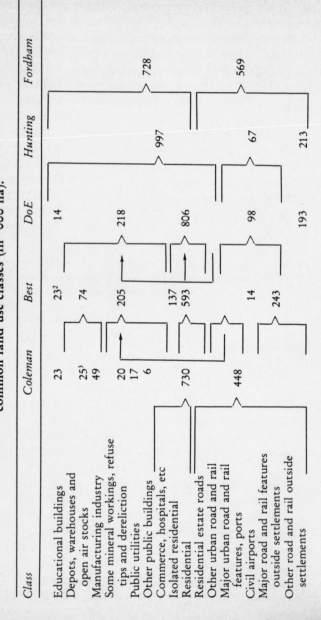

Class	Coleman	Best	DoE	Hunting	Fordham
Educational buildings	23	23[2]	14		
Depots, warehouses and open air stocks	25[3]	74			
Manufacturing industry	49				
Some mineral workings, refuse tips and dereliction	20	205	218		
Public utilities	17				
Other public buildings	6				728
Commerce, hospitals, etc		137		997	
Isolated residential		593	806		
Residential	730				
Residential estate roads					
Other urban road and rail					
Major urban road and rail features, ports	448	14	98	67	569
Civil airports		243			
Major road and rail features outside settlements			193	213	
Other road and rail outside settlements					

Table 4 : II – continued

	Coleman	Best	DoE	Hunting	Fordham
Allotments	32	⎫	⎫	⎫	32
Open space	177	201²	193	197	177
Urban total	1,527	1,490	1,522	1,474	1,506
Urban percentage	10.1	9.9	10.1	9.8	10.0

1. See text for the numerous adjustments to the results published by these surveys.
2. Educational buildings are assumed to have been as in Coleman. Best's extra 22,000 ha is assumed to be playing fields and has been transferred to open space.
3. Best's industrial category is assumed to include depots, warehouses and open air material stocks. Accepting Best's figure, 25,000 ha is therefore transferred from Coleman's commerce and residential.

Table 4 : III
Summary of Table II (' 000 ha)

Major class	Coleman	Best	DoE	Hunting	Fordham
Built up properties	870	842	881	829	728
Transport land[1]	448	448	448	448	569
Urban open space[1]	209	201	193	197	209
Urban total	1,527	1,490	1,522	1,474	1,506

1. Estimates are identical only due to the assumptions explained in the text.

1978: 3-4), which has to be transferred from open space; boundary generalisation and omission of isolated settlements partially cancelled each other out, leaving half of Best's isolated settlements (i.e. 70,000 ha) to be added to residential; 20,000 ha were transferred to open space, because grass areas of less than 5 ha were included in residential; of Best's 257,000 ha of transport land outside settlements (1981: 61), only 50,000 ha, plus 14,000 ha airports, was actually recorded, leaving 193,000 ha to be added; Best's figure of 126,000 ha for urban growth between 1961/62 and 1968/69 must be subtracted from the five classes in proportion to their areas. Many of the quantities chosen are guesses.

The latest land use survey of England and Wales was conducted in 1984. The DoE and the Countryside Commission contracted Hunting Surveys and Consultants Ltd to obtain statistically reliable information on post-war change in the distribution of landscape features (Deane 1986: 346). Twelve thousand air photographs taken around 1947, 1969 and 1980 were obtained for a stratified random sample of sites covering 2.4% of the area. The quality of interpretation was checked on the ground at 340 sites, and also by satellite data for 1984. Five major classes of ground cover were delineated, the fifth of which, 'other land', comprised bare rock, sand, and 'developed land', the latter being divided into five categories: built-up, open space, transport routes, quarries, and derelict. Larger scale photographs than in the Developed Areas survey were used, giving a resolution level of 0.25 ha. Mapping was at 1:25,000, and the maps were digitised for area measurement. However, the measurement of only 74,000 ha for transport routes in 1969, less than in the DA survey, strongly suggests that, once again, most isolated dwellings and rural transport land escaped the net.

Apart from the inclusion of all recorded mineral workings and derelict land, the developed land definition in the final report (Hunting 1986: volume 2, Appendix D, 120-130) is comparable with Best's. Urban growth of 126,000 ha is therefore subtracted from the 1969 data; Best's isolated dwellings and rural transport, minus 20,000 ha and 30,000 ha, respectively — arbitrarily assumed to be actually recorded — are added; 20,000 ha is added to open space for allotments, which, according to the definitions, 'should usually be part of open country'; and another arbitrary 20,000 ha is added because playing fields and parks are only 'usually included in Urban Limit'.

It can be seen from the bottom line of Table 4:II that Best's conclusion is justified if the numerous foregoing assumptions are anywhere near the mark. It can also be seen that dividing this 10% of the surface area of England and Wales into its constituent parts poses yet more problems.

The Urban Sub-Divisions — England and Wales, 1961

The most obvious problem with sub-dividing the urban area is the contradiction over transport land. Fordham's estimate is 27% higher than Coleman's — a matter of 121,000 ha, or 8% of the urban area. Both sampled 6" OS maps for the most part, so how could this have occurred?

The most likely explanation is that the contradiction is more apparent than real, because the difference lies well within the bounds of statistical error. Fordham noted that the larger part of his transport land lay outside 'built up areas'. This meant that it was dealt with by his survey of 6" maps rather than by his survey of the 25" maps which he used for obtaining the division of urban land uses within administratively urban areas. He wrote of the 6" survey that 'the sampling density was not intended to permit accurate measurement of the fifteen uses, but to achieve good accuracy for the UR [urban in rural areas] estimate' (1974: 36). Accuracy being related to the size of the class measured, the urban total was obviously more accurate than its constituent parts.

Whatever the class size, accuracy also depends on the number of points sampled. Only 9,000 point observations were made for the Rural Districts of the UK, whereas Coleman must have made nearly 130,000 for those in England and Wales alone. Within Urban Districts about 15,000 and 23,000 observations were made, respectively (though the latter were still on 6" maps, which, if anything, overstate urban transport land). 100,000 of Fordham's observations were made on one inch maps for the purpose of measuring the urban aggregate alone, not its constituent parts, for which the one inch maps are inadequate.

Fordham's other two umbrella categories — buildings and open land — occur mainly in Urban Districts, and errors in the 6" survey must have had less effect on them. It is clear that his transport category must have been the least accurate of the three. His generalisation for all three that 'it is likely that there is a two-thirds chance of the true figure being within 20% of the estimate' would, therefore, appear to have been optimistic as regards transport land. Coleman's estimate was 21% less, and that was also liable to error (though lower, according to the standard errors presented, by an order of magnitude).

It is worth noting at this point that Hunting and Anderson claimed sampling accuracies of the same order as Fordham's. Also the accuracy of the photo interpretation by both Hunting and the DoE was claimed to range between 90 and 99% (Deane 1986: 347; Rhind and Hudson 1980: 79).

Returning to Table 4:II, the difficulty of assessing the various classifications is obvious. Table 4:III is presented as an attempt to make that task easier.

In view of the foregoing discussion of statistical methods, we decided to adopt the transport measurement from the Second Land Utilisation Survey. The figures could be reworked using Fordham's data or a compromise estimate. However, given the lower estimate, certain deductions follow.

First, Fordham's built up properties must be increased by 121,000 ha — he measured very little non-garden open space and rural districts have smaller urban open space components anyway (Best 1981: 68) so open land would hardly have been affected. In round figures, the picture from the five surveys now looks like this:

Built up properties	850,000 ha
Transport land	450,000 ha
Urban open space	200,000 ha
Urban total	1,500,000 ha

(Of course, Fordham's extra transport land may have been partially at the expense of rural land. The urban area may easily have been exaggerated by, say, 60,000 ha. But then his adjusted results would have been further out of line.)

Second, the transport sub-divisions may be roughly quantified, in the order in which they appear in Table 4 : II, as follows: 100, 60, 31, 14, 43, 200 ('000 ha).

Third, a means of reconciling the difference between Best and the DoE over the residential area presents itself. If most of the 60,000 ha approximately of 'other urban road and rail' belongs in the DoE's 'predominantly residential' category, then two-thirds of the difference melts away. The residential area shorn of roads becomes roughly 650,000 ha, and the rest of the built up properties, roughly 200,000 ha.

Urban Growth in England and Wales, 1961-1985

Having analysed the position in 1961 in some detail we must now attempt to bring it up to date. Margaret Anderson has carried the urban total up to 1985 by continuing Best's analysis of the annual returns of farmland transfers to urban use (The Inner City Commission 1987: 32). By this method the 1985 urban area is reckoned to be 1.78m ha or 11.8% of England and Wales.

This result may be checked against the Hunting survey, which was aimed at monitoring landscape change. The results cannot be compared directly due to the adjustments that have to be made to bring the urban coverage into line. But in the analysis above, 23% (300,000 ha) was added to the estimated 1961 equivalent of the 1969 measurement, and if 23% is added to the 1980 measurement, a figure of 1.796m ha is produced, as against Best's/Anderson's 1.756m ha (Best and Anderson 1984 : 22).

The categories covered by the adjustment to the 1961 area, however, would not have grown at the same rate (i.e. by 66,000 ha) as the rest of the urban area. They consisted of isolated dwellings and farmsteads and transport outside settlements. The planning system probably kept the former fairly static, and the contraction of the railways probably counterbalanced the extension of the motorways. A third of the 22% growth may have occurred, which would bring the Hunting and Best estimates into line.

Fordham gave it as his judgement on Best's use of the annual returns from all farmers that 'The procedure has consistency and continuity. For this reason it may be regarded as having fair accuracy' (Fordham 1974: 51).

The Urban Composition in 1985

Regarding the composition of the urban area in 1985, one has to look for clues as to how the 1961 picture may have changed. The DoE's trial project on monitoring land use change has produced data for 1985 and 1986, and unlike the Hunting project is particularly strong on the urban sector. But the time span is narrow and not necessarily representative, the coverage is for England alone, and there is the usual problem of having to merge somewhat incompatible land use classifications.

In Table 4 : IV the land use classes of Tables 4 : II and 4 : III and of the DoE project are roughly consolidated. Residential estate roads have been included in residential, and utilities with transport. To achieve an approximation to the latter's 'community services' category, hospitals have been extracted from their place in column 2 of Table 4 : II and combined with educational buildings and other public buildings. For this purpose the area of the National Health Service given by Dowrick for 1972/3 was used (Dowrick 1974). Fortunately, government offices are combined with industry and commerce in both classifications.

Another problem was the treatment of 'waste land'. This class has no equivalent in Table 4 : II, derelict land being only a small proportion of it. It was decided that, as it was included in the other classes and only an indication of the growth of those classes was needed, waste land could be safely subtracted from the DoE figures.

The 280,000 ha addition to urban land between 1961 and 1985 was then allocated to each class in the same proportion as its share of the addition to urban land in 1985 and 1986, producing its calculated area for 1985.

The Area of Commercial Land

The land use classes of most interest to this study — the highest value ones — are also the smallest and hence the least accurately measured at the national scale. In fact, no attempt has yet been made, or will be in the foreseeable future, to measure the area of commercial land in the country. However, at a more local level the

Table 4 : IV
Estimated change in urban land uses, 1961-1985

Class	(1) 1961 stock ('000 ha)	(2) 1961 share (%)	(3) Share of 1985-1986 urban growth (%)	(4) % in (3) applied to urban growth 1961-1985 ('000 ha)	(5) 1985 stock, (1) + (4) ('000 ha)	(6) 1985 share (%)
Community services	53	3.5	4.0	11.2	64.2	3.6
Industry and commerce	131	8.7	8.9	24.9	155.9	8.8
Residential	750	50.0	66.5	186.2	936.2	52.6
Transport and utilities	366	24.4	11.2	31.4	397.4	22.3
Outdoor recreation	200	13.3	9.4	26.3	226.3	12.7
Total	1500	100.0	100.0	280	1780	100.0

Source: Tables 4:II and 4:III above; Dowrick 1974; DoE 1986: Table 1; DoE 1987: Table 1.

Table 4 : V

The area of commercial and public buildings as a percentage of urban area in several local studies

	London Borough of Tower Hamlets (1977)	Leeds (developed) area, 1976)	Merseyside County (1976)	Thames Estuary (1972)	Cleveland County (1978)	Surrey (1978)	Buckinghamshire (1977)
1. Public buildings and institutions	7.3	8.8	3.8	45.3	3.9	3.5	3.5
2. Commerce	11.6	4.3	3.4		3.2	2.8	2.5
3. Residential	11	40	38		33	49	40
4. % of area urbanised	100	100	56	49	40	29	16
5. '000 people per km²	7.3	5.7	2.3	—	0.9	0.6	0.3
6. Row 4 divided by row 5	14	18	24	—	44	48	53

Sources: Dickinson and Shaw 1982:346; Rhind and Hudson 1980: 140-141; Second Land Utilisation Survey of Britain, King's College, London; Pears Cyclopaedia 1980.

obstacles are not so great and there have been a number of studies which have thrown light on this facet of urban areas.

The Second Land Utilisation Survey's re-surveys of the 1970s, for example, became more urban orientated and distinguished commercial areas and all public buildings from residential land. Dr Coleman and Mrs Janet Shaw have kindly made available from the Survey's computer files at King's College, London, hitherto unpublished data on these land uses in Surrey and Buckinghamshire. In Table 4 : V this is combined with results from their surveys of Merseyside and Tower Hamlets, and with information from the Cleveland County Planning Department and the School of Geography at the University of Leeds.

In order to assist interpretation of the table, the sets of figures have been ranked according to the degree to which they focus on central areas, as measured by population density and percentage of the study area urbanised. Obviously studies which are specifically of central business districts will include more commercial land than those which have a wider focus. An attempt must be made to decide which data set is the most representative of England and Wales as a whole.

The population density of England and Wales is 330 persons/km^2, and roughly 12% of its surface is urbanised. From an inspection of Table 4 : V it would seem that Buckinghamshire might be the choice, but its population density looks rather low in relation to its urban area, suggesting an under-representation of larger urban centres. If the percentage of area urbanised is divided by population density (in thousands per square kilometre), as in the table, then England and Wales' 36.3 is somewhere between Merseyside and Cleveland. It is proposed that this position is correct, and that public buildings occupy 3.8% of the urban area of England and Wales and commercial buildings 3.3%. Janet Shaw does point out that there is 'a slight difference in mapping technique' between the Merseyside and Surrey/Bucks surveys, but the percentages chosen leave an area for industrial land which allows for reasonable growth since 1961.

'Commerce' is taken as comprising roughly the same categories as appear under that heading in the rating statistics: shops, offices, public houses, hotels, restaurants, warehouses, commercial garages

Table 4 : VI

The Composition of Commercial Land in Three Local Studies

	Wholesale/storage (%)	Retail (%)	Office (%)	Total ('000 ha)
Cleveland	68.8	28.2	3.1	785
Merseyside	27.3	69.7	3.0	1,238
Leeds	43.3	48.4	8.4	548

Source: As in Table 4 : V.

Table 4 : VII

Urban land uses in England and Wales in 1961 and 1985,
extended to Great Britain in 1985

Class	England and Wales 1961		England and Wales 1985		Great Britain 1985	
	('000 ha)	(%)	('000 ha)	(%)	('000 ha)	(%)
Commerce	34	2.25	40	2.25	46	2.25
Industry and warehouses	73	4.9	93	5.2	106	5.2
Public utilities	17	1.1	20	1.1	22	1.1
Public buildings and institutions	58	3.9	68	3.8	77	3.8
Some mineral workings/dereliction	20	1.3	20	1.1	22	1.1
Residential	650	43.3	810	45.5	920	45.5
Residential estate roads	100	6.7	126	7.1	144	7.1
Other urban road and rail, ports	91	6.1	99	5.6	113	5.6
Road and rail outside settlements, civil airports	257	17.1	278	15.6	343	16.9
Open space	200	13.3	226	12.7	230	11.4
Total urban	1,500	100.0	1,780	100.0	2,023	100.0
Urban as % of total area		9.9		11.8		8.8

and other minor land uses. Boarding houses and lock-up garages form an indeterminate area as far as this study is concerned on the border between commerce and housing.

Warehouses are usually situated on industrial estates and valued accordingly. They should therefore be classified separately from shops and offices, as in Table 4:II. Table 4:VI sets out the information on these uses in the studies cited above. It is probable that Cleveland County (which includes Teeside) has an unusually large proportion of land devoted to storage of material stocks for heavy industry, and that the county of Merseyside is more representative of the whole country than is the city of Leeds. 32% has therefore been taken as the proportion of commercial land to be classed as industrial, which means that commercial land occupies 2.25% of the urban area and industry and storage 5.2%.

Table 4:VII applies these percentages to Table 4:IV assuming no change between 1961 and 1985, and sub-divides transport and utilities on the same assumption. It also extends the results to cover Scotland, which is yet another hazardous undertaking.

The Urban Area of Scotland

Only Fordham and Best have ventured into this uncharted territory, the former relying particularly on his 6″ maps, the latter on 'essentially proxy figures derived from English and Welsh material' (Best 1981: 63). Predictably, Fordham's Scottish urban total for 1961, 59% of which was transport, was 12% higher than Best's. An over-measurement of transport land might not have affected the UK total, but it would have affected its regions, especially Scotland, Wales and Northern Ireland. Fordham gave the likely two-thirds confidence limits around his Scottish figure of 225,000 ha as plus or minus 31-35,000 ha (1974: 45, 47). Best's 199,000 ha, therefore, would seem to command a modicum of credibility.

Given Best's estimate, it only remains to bring it up to date. If the same relation between Scotland and its neighbours held in 1985 as in 1981 and 1971 (Best and Anderson 1984: 22) then the urban total was 243,000 ha. Looking at Best's division of this land between different settlement categories (1981: 61) there would appear to be no reason for expecting a markedly different percentage of valuable commercial land. A top heavy hierarchy was counter-balanced by the wide expanse of transport land; the index number in the bottom line of Table 4 : V would have been 46.7. An adjustment has, however, been made to reflect the contrasting amounts of transport land and urban open space in Scotland.

The Need for a Land Use Monitoring System

Table 4 : VII closes this investigation. But it will have become apparent by now that unlike in the average whodunnit all the loose ends have not been tied up. The very need for this inquiry has shown that the official process of monitoring the impact of an official function — land use planning — falls far short of what is required.

Rhind and Hudson (1980: 17) have summarised the difficulties of implementing an ideal monitoring system. Collecting data in a form detailed and flexible enough to be suitable for all potential uses is an expensive process. It would be necessary for the State to create a standard spatial referencing system and a standard land use classification, as called for by the Chorley Committee. The basic spatial unit measured would have to be small enough to be uniform both in form and function, and the monitoring process would have to be continuous. In this way whatever aggregations of the units might be required — towns, counties, regions, etc. — might be compared over time and space. Many of the elements of the system, however, are already in place at the local authority level.

The task is one that most national governments have not undertaken. It is clearly one that in the interests of better planning and better use of scarce resources the Government of Britain should be able, and willing, to undertake.

5

Farm, Wood and Forest Land

DUNCAN PICKARD

IN ESTIMATING the value of agricultural land in Great Britain, the market price of land without buildings sold with vacant possession in 1985 has been taken as representative of the value for the whole country. However, less than 2% of the total agricultural land was sold in that year and it is impossible to be sure that the value estimated in this way is truly representative, but in the absence of more comprehensive data on land values, this is the most reliable approach.

Since it is the value of the land only which is sought, the commonly quoted figures for the value of farmland cannot be used because these include the value of farm houses and buildings. For England and Wales, separate figures are available for the price of land sold without buildings. The ratio between the price of land only and the price of land with and without buildings is 0.9 for England.[1] This ratio has been used to estimate the price of land only in Scotland from the price of land with and without buildings, because separate figures are not available for Scotland.

A considerable proportion of all agricultural land sold in England and Wales in 1985 with vacant possession was land only (55,875 ha out of a total of 127,209 ha) (MAFF 1986a: 6). However, 80% of the transactions in land only were of areas less than 20 ha, and 73% of the total area sold was in units of less than 50 ha. Small lots are usually sold at a higher price per hectare than large lots and this may lead to over-estimation of the value of the total agricultural area. (It should be noted that areas sold which are less than 5 ha are not included in these statistics.)

1 Agricultural land

Method A

The price paid for farmland without buildings sold with vacant possession in 1984-5 in England was £3,466/ha. In Wales it was £2,461/ha (MAFF 1986a: 4, 5). The estimated price of land in Scotland was £1,413/ha[2]. These prices reflect the fact that Wales and Scotland have a much greater proportion of poor quality mountainous farmland than does England (see Table 5 : III).

The area of agricultural land in Great Britain has been calculated from *Social Trends* (CSO 1987 : 160) and the relevant data used to estimate the total value are set out in Table 5 : I.

Table 5 : I

Agricultural land, 1985: Method A

Country	Area (ha)	Price per ha (£)	Total value (£ bn)
England	9,723,750	3,466	33.702
Wales	1,651,200	2,461	4.064
Scotland	6,320,560	1,413	8.931
			46.697

Method B

An alternative method of estimating land value is to consider the value of farmland according to its productive potential. The Ministry of Agriculture has classified farmland into five grades, based on such features as soil type, climate and elevation. Grade 1 is the most productive and is considered capable of producing any type of crop; Grade 5 is the poorest land and is usually suitable only for sheep farming or for forestry. In Wales only 0.2% of the agricultural land is Grade 1 whilst 36% is Grade 5; in East Anglia comparable figures are 10.9% of Grade 1 land and only 0.1% of Grade 5 land (MAFF 1974: 14).

The Ministry of Agriculture provides figures for the price of land sold with vacant possession in each grade (MAFF 1987b: Table 5).

Unfortunately these figures are the average prices paid both for land only and for land with buildings, and therefore have been recalculated (using the ratio of 0.9) to give an estimate of the price of land only for England and Wales. Comparable figures for Scotland are not available.

The proportions of land in England and Wales in each grade, the average price of each grade and the total values are shown in Table 5:II. This figure of £38.511 bn is close to that calculated for England and Wales of £37.766 bn (derived from Table 5:I), which increases confidence in that estimate of land value.

Table 5 : II
Agricultural land, 1985: Method B

Grade	Proportion %	Area ha	Average price £/ha	Value £bn
1	2.8	318,499	5,417	1.725
2	14.6	1,660,743	4,597	7.634
3	48.9	5,562,350	3,864	21.493
4	19.7	2,240,865	2,952	6.615
5	14.0	1,592,493	659	1.049
Total				38.516

Method C

The Ministry of Agriculture provides statistics for the amounts of arable, grassland, rough grazing, woodland and other land on farms in Great Britain (MAFF 1986b: 4, 5, 6). In the absence of official statistics for the price of these categories of land, we have taken as reasonable estimates of the land price in each category: arable land £4,000/ha, permanent grassland £3,000/ha, rough grazing £740/ha, woodland £740/ha and other land £3,000/ha[3].

The value of agricultural land in Great Britain using these figures is shown in Table 5:III, which gives an estimated total value of £45.643 bn and average prices/ha for each country of: England £3,224, Wales £2,407 and Scotland £1,592. The estimated total value of £45.643 bn is similar to that calculated earlier in Table 5:I of £46.697 bn.

Table 5 : III
Agricultural land, 1985: Method C

	England		Wales		Scotland	
	ha	*Value £bn*	*ha*	*Value £bn*	*ha*	*Value £bn*
Arable land	5,347,628	21.391	264,682	1.059	1,133,877	4.535
Permanent grassland	3,064,331	9.193	854,086	2.562	580,392	1.741
Rough grazings	1,186,670	0.878	529,252	0.392	4,172,092	3.087
Woodland	192,972	0.143	32,522	0.024	74,985	0.055
Other land	143,947	0.432	13,360	0.040	37,025	0.111
Total	9,937,548	32.037	1,693,902	4.077	5,988,375	9.529

Land Values in the National Balance Sheet
Attempts to estimate land values from the *UK National Acounts*
balance sheet for 1985 have not been successful. It is not possible
to derive a figure for the vacant possession value of land only,
because the prices listed in the balance sheet are for tenanted
and owner-occupied land and buildings. The figures also refer to
the whole of the United Kingdom and must be considerably lower
than the total vacant possession value of the land, because they
show that the total value of the farmland and buildings in the UK is
only £37 bn. Approximately 40% of the farmland in Great Britain is
tenanted (MAFF 1986b: 10) and the price of land only sold subject
to a tenancy was 70% of the price of land sold with vacant
possession in 1985 (MAFF 1986a: 6).

2   Forest and woodland

The total area of forest and woodland in Great Britain is 2,165,000
ha (*Social Trends* 15, 1985: Table 9.16) and of this area 300,479 ha is
woodland on farms (MAFF 1986b: 4, 5, 6). Most of the forest land
is in upland Scotland and Wales, and the average price of vacant
land for forestry in 1986 was £740/ha (IRVO Spring 1987: 75).
The value of the land occupied by woodland on farms has been
taken as this price which gives a total value of forest and woodland
of £1.602 bn.

3   Conclusion: Capital Values

The total value of agricultural land, woodland and forestland in
Great Britain in 1985 was estimated to be £48.299 bn (£46.697 bn +
£1.602 bn).

4   Farm Rents

The average rent of farmland with a rent change in England and
Wales was about £93/ha in 1985. This figure is for the rent of farms
and therefore includes farmhouses and buildings. It is not possible
to derive the rent applicable to land only from this figure.
   The only published figures for the rent of land alone are those for

summer grazing (MAFF 1987c). In 1986 the average rent paid for this land was £169/ha, but most of it was grassland in Grade 3 and was let for the period between April and November. Why does it attract a higher rent than farmland with buildings for the whole year?

Taking the average sale value of tenanted farmland (with buildings) in England and Wales of £2,735/ha and the average rent of £93/ha, the rate of return is 3.4%, but taking the average value of land alone of £3,340 and the rent paid for summer grazing of £169/ha, the rate of return is 5.1%.

NOTES

1   The average price of land sold with vacant possession, with and without buildings in England in 1985 was £3,871/ha (MAFF 1987a: 77). The price of land only was £3,466/ha (MAFF 1986a: 4) giving a ratio of 0.9.

2   For Scotland the average vacant possession price of land with and without buildings was £1,570 (MAFF 1987a: 77), which when multiplied by 0.9 gives an estimated value of land for Scotland of £1,413/ha.

3   'Other land' refers to land on farms which is covered by houses and buildings, farmyards and farm roads and has been given an estimated price similar to that of permanent grassland. Although some of the 'other land' may be worth considerably more than this price, the area involved is small and the total value of agricultural land would not be much affected if a higher price were used.

6
Residential Land

FRANCIS SMITH

THIS CHAPTER is an attempt to derive the best estimate of the value of all the land used or allocated for dwellings in 1985. We are not necessarily concerned about the precise total area of land involved at this stage (a surprising small 4% of the country, according to Table 4: VII). Much of the information available to us relates to numbers of dwellings and the plots on which they stand without any direct recognition of the area of those plots. Analysis of such information provides us with a semi-independent check of an estimate obtained by multiplying spatial area and average unit value.

Our main sources of information have been two official publications: the Department of the Environment's (with other government departments) *Housing and Construction Statistics 1975-1985 GREAT BRITAIN* (DoE/SDD/WO 1986); and the Inland Revenue Valuation Office's Autumn 1985 *Property Market Report*. It is in the former that the importance of the emphasis on the number of dwellings becomes apparent — there is no other consistently reliable database covering the whole country. The latter, however, provides us with more appropriate information on land values, and this is applied first to the official numbers of dwellings and then to the national area of housing land worked out in Chapter 4.

Definition of a Dwelling

DoE/SDD/WO (1986: 150) contains the following definitions to which we have adhered:

A dwelling is a building or any part of a building which forms a separate and self-contained set of premises designed to be occupied by a single family.

A flat is a dwelling forming part of a building from some other part of which it is divided horizontally. For the purpose of statistics of new building old persons flatlets (one or two room flats with certain shared facilities) are counted as separate one-bedroomed flats although they are not entirely self-contained. Flats include maisonettes, which are flats containing more than one storey.

A house is a dwelling which is not a flat. Houses include single storey bungalows.

Estimates of the total dwelling stock are critical to the method of calculation used and therefore the method employed by the Department of the Environment is noted in full:

Estimates of the total dwelling stock, stock changes and the tenure distribution are based on data from the Censuses of Population, with adjustments for numeration errors and for definitional changes. English figures are based on figures from the 1971 and 1981 censuses. Estimates for Wales and Scotland prior to 1981 are based on 1971 census data and are not strictly comparable with those for later years which are based on 1981 census data.

The 1981 census did not include a direct count of dwellings but estimates have been made using the information about access which was recorded for each 'household space' (the living accommodation occupied or intended to be occupied by one household). The method used was to take the number of self-contained household spaces in permanent buildings, each of which must by definition correspond to a separate dwelling, and add to that figure an allowance for shared dwellings by assuming that on average 100 'not self-contained' household spaces are equivalent to 30 separate dwellings (20 in some areas of London where sharing is prevalent). Since only a very small proportion of dwellings are shared the dwelling stock estimate is not very sensitive to the number of household spaces assumed per shared dwelling: the maximum possible error on this account represents less than 0.5% of total dwelling stock nationally and only about 1% for London, the area most affected. (All household spaces which are not in permanent buildings are assumed to be self-contained dwellings.)

The tenure categories are as defined in the census reports. In Scotland dwellings rented from local authorities include those rented from the Scottish Special Housing Association. 'Other' tenures include dwellings rented with farms or business premises, those occupied by virtue of employment and those rented from housing associations.

Estimates of dwelling stock by tenure from censuses involve

additional assumptions particularly in respect of dwellings where usual residents are not present on census night (eg, absent households, vacant dwellings) and are therefore liable to wider margins of error than the estimates of total stock (1986:154-5).

Account is taken of gains in conversions and losses by demolition and slum clearance.

Categories of Dwelling Land

There are four categories which will be included in this analysis, namely: privately owned; privately rented; local authority owned; and vacant plots intended for dwellings.

The most reliable information relates to private ownership. Local authority land is the most difficult to value and that for which the least hard fact is available. Since there is no recognised way of determining the value of dwelling land by local authorities themselves, estimates were made.

DoE/SDD/WO (1986: Table 10.1) contains information on land sold with planning permission for housing in the private sector. This information is derived from the Inland Revenue Valuation Office, which also publishes its own summary of the opinions of District Valuers. Finally, the Nationwide Building Society records site value estimates made by surveyors, using the 'residual method', during routine valuation of houses for mortgage security purposes.

The value of anything in the market place is what someone is prepared to pay for it. The greater the number of similar transactions there are the more reliable the indication of current values. For housing there is a buoyant and widespread market, with a large amount of publicly available detail.

The Press abounds with horror stories about rises in the prices of properties: *The Sunday Times* (3 January, 1988) states that in London 'an ordinary Victorian terrace house last year increased in value by £137 a day'. This is primarily an increase in land value. The increase is fastest and greatest in the South East, but it is also occurring in desirable areas in other parts of the country. The commuting boundaries for London have been ever widening, related largely to travelling convenience; as a consequence house prices are increasing rapidly in entirely new areas like Grantham.

The desire for positional wealth has increased the demand for country mansions, manor houses and large properties often scorned in earlier years; this, for example has made the Cotswolds a very expensive area.

The rate of increase in values was not as great in 1985 as in the ensuing years. Apart from the fact that it was the latest year for which complete figures were available when study commenced, this makes it a suitable (i.e. relatively normal) year for investigaion.

Private Sector House Building Land: The DoE's Data

DoE/SDD/WO (1986: 105-109) gives details of transactions for the purchase of land designated for private and public sector housing and consisting of four or more plots. The explanatory notes are as follows:

> Data on transactions for land intended to be used for housing is taken from a return completed by Inland Revenue District Valuers using information taken from stamp duty records (the *Particulars Delivered*) and other sources. Table 10.2 provides summary information on all the transactions reported from 1981. Table 10.1 provides information for transactions used in the construction of the index of housing land prices. These are, broadly, restricted to private sector purchase of sites with planning permission for a known number of plots (i.e. dwellings in the case of flats) (p. 155).

These tables are a direct indication of the value of house building land, as they relate to site value alone. However, only Table 10.1 includes average figures and may therefore be used for the calculation of totals. This table, which contains only those transactions suitable for the construction of a constant average building density price index, will produce conservative estimates for three reasons:

1   It does not include building sites for under four dwellings, which, especially those for one dwelling, normally fetch higher prices.

2   It does not include 'sites where the housing density is exceptionally high, [i.e.] above ... 60 dwellings per acre in London, 30 in the rest of the South East and in most of the conurbations,

and 18 elsewhere' (Evans 1974:XIV). Such sites tend to be the highest value sites of all.

3   The figures must on average represent the start rather than the mid-point of the year, as a footnote to the table states: 'Transactions are reported on average about 9 weeks after the completion of sales. The lag between agreement of price and completion varies considerably, but about three months is thought to be typical.'

Table 6:I gives the total number of dwellings for each region and country together with the number of plots purchased in 1985 (already having planning permission and in transactions consisting of four plots or more) and their 'simple average' and median prices per plot. The number of plots purchased bears a similar ratio to the number of existing plots in each case except two, and in two cases there were exceptionally high purchase prices. The anomalies are:

East Midlands: there was an exceptionally high number of purchases for this particular year but the prices were not distorted.

The South East — Greater London: prices were exceptionally high and there was a very low number of purchases. This is not unexpected and is only noted because it has a significant influence on the total figure.

Rest of the South East: there was an average amount of land purchased but the prices were exceptionally high (£15,000 per plot against an overall average of £8,315 in England and Wales).

The significantly higher prices per plot and per hectare are clearly seen in the average figures for the South East. The higher priced plots are not analysed in the published figures except in the totals and therefore the incidence of higher priced areas within regions or countries are not disclosed. However, the main influence is within the South East and therefore the use of averages per region and per country should not produce a large distortion.

Before moving on it is worth looking briefly at the comparison between purchases of land with planning permission, as given in DoE/SDD/WO (1986) Table 10.1, and the combined figure which

Table 6 : I
Selected DoE housing statistics for 1985

Region or country	Stock of dwellings (Dec. 1985)	Plots purchased	Price per plot with planning permission	
			Average	Median
North	1,238	850	3,798	3,500
Yorkshire and Humberside	1,944	2,443	4,165	3,250
East Midlands	1,537	4,332	3,767	2,427
Greater London	2,805	1,542	14,914	11,833
Rest of South East	4,065	6,170	15,339	13,541
East Anglia	796	1,505	7,183	5,000
South West	1,824	2,892	8,222	6,643
West Midlands	2,004	3,220	7,318	5,447
North West	2,518	3,047	4,817	4,700
Wales	1,120	838	3,563	3,191
England and Wales	19,851	26,839	8,315	5,375
Scotland	2,045	—	3,762*	NA
Great Britain	21,896	—	8,053*	NA

* Estimated from Building Societies' average new house price and assuming land value to be 11% of the total as in North (*Regional Trends* 1987:66). A notional 1600 plots for Scotland has been assumed to enable an approximate figure for Great Britain to be calculated.

includes land designated for private housing but without planning permission, and for public housing, as given in Table 10.2 (see Table 6:II). Table 10.2 also gives the spread in prices paid per hectare for each region and country as indicated by the lower and upper quartiles and the median (see Figure 6:I).

Figure 6 : I
Spread of housing land prices in England and Wales,
early 1985

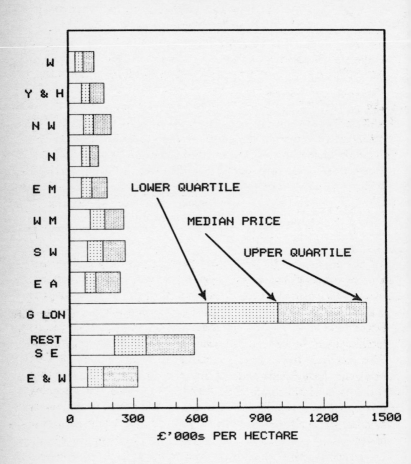

Table 6 : II
The DoE's median housing land prices in early 1985

Region or Country	Hectares purchased		Median price (£'000/ha)	
	Private only, with planning permission	*All sectors, with and without planning permission*	*Private only, with planning permission*	*All sectors, with and without planning permission*
North	37	125	92	100
Yorks. and Humber.	94	177	86	102
East Midlands	177	431	69	108
East Anglia	82	223	95	125
Greater London	28	81	771	983
Rest of South East	269	589	329	361
South West	125	289	172	160
West Midlands	143	359	131	170
North West	132	289	94	118
Wales	40	161	74	72
England and Wales	1,125	2,725	129	158

Only in the South West and Wales is the median price per hectare including land without planning permission lower than that for land with planning permission. In both areas the upper quartile is also exceptionally high relative to the lower quartile. These two facts would suggest that there is a limited amount of land which is fetching much higher prices, presumably in certain desirable areas. This relatively high upper quartile is also apparent in the East Midlands, East Anglia and the South West, which suggests that those parts within commuting distance/time of London are going up in price more rapidly. This distortion does not show in Greater London where all the prices are very high and the differentials are lower.

The generally higher prices for land without planning permission imply either speculation, the desire of builders or developers to build up land banks, or their anticipation of building in greater densities.

The Value of Land Associated with the Purchase of New Dwellings through the Nationwide Building Society

The Nationwide Anglia Building Society (formerly the Nationwide Building Society) publishes quarterly the regional and UK weighted average prices of the houses on which it provides mortgages. Their UK average prices for new dwellings in 1985 were about 10% higher than the equivalent figures (i.e. at mortgage approval stage) given by the Building Societies Association (Fleming and Nellis 1987 : 28).

The Nationwide Anglia also keeps a list of unweighted (i.e. simple) average prices of new properties and their average site values. In the 4th quarter of 1985 the average UK new property price was about 16% higher than the BSA figure, but this bias was partially offset by the fact that the average price of the dwellings for which building societies *and* banks provided loans was 7.5% higher than the average price of the dwellings for which building societies alone provided loans (DoE/SDD/WO 1986 : 110). At the same time the average UK new house site value was about 40% higher than the GB average given in Table 6 : I. There are two obvious reasons why this should be so:

1   Site value, here, includes the costs of site preparation and servicing. Taking off 18% for these (*The Estates Gazette*, August 22, 1987), notwithstanding Hallet's claim that they amount to half of all site values (1979 : 86), leaves it 12% higher.

2   The Table 6 : I figure actually applies to the start of 1985. The Nationwide figure is about 18% lower than the figure for the start of 1986.

Thus, the Nationwide Anglia data appears generally to confirm the DoE data, but its utility is reduced by the fact that it is not strictly limited to site values. As would be expected, the inclusion of the cost of site works, which is fairly uniform regionally, serves to lower the regional variation of the proportion of site values to total values (21%-29%) compared with the DoE data (11%-34%) given in *Regional Trends* (1987 : 66).

The District Valuers' Assessment of Land for Residential Development

The Valuation Office's six-monthly *Property Market Report* has a chart which summarises the views of the 160 District Valuers on the value of the land used for residential development in their areas. The information is presented in the form of average values by region of three categories of site — small sites, bulk land and sites for flats or maisonettes. The averages of these categories for England and Wales are also calculated, excluding London.

For purposes of comparison with the DoE data it would seem to be necessary to look at bulk land only. The England and Wales average value per hectare for small sites as at 1 October 1985 (IRVO no. 44:19) was 21% higher than for bulk land, and the average for sites for flats or maisonettes was 51% higher. If London had been included both might have been expected to be even higher relatively. Despite their exclusion, however, the District Valuers' still managed to produce an England and Wales average without London of £267,000/ha compared to the DoE's average with London of £198,000/ha.

This huge gulf between the figures can be entirely explained by differences in temporal and spatial coverage:

1   There is roughly an eight month gap between the effective mid-point of the DoE's '1985' period and the effective date of the District Valuers' assessment. Taking two-thirds of the increase in the DoE average between 1985 and 1986 to close the gap raises the average by 21% to £239,857/ha.

2   The DoE average excludes land bought without planning permission for housing and land bought by the public sector. There were nearly twice as many of these transactions alone recorded by the DoE, in its Table 10.2, as there were transactions used for calculating the average, in its Table 10.1. The median in Table 10.2 was 22.5% greater than the median in Table 10.1. Assuming that the average can also be raised by the same percentage gives us a final adjusted average for England and Wales of £293,825/ha. The District Valuers' average, including London (deducible from Figure 6:II), is £293,707/ha.

Figure 6 : II
Housing land prices in England and Wales

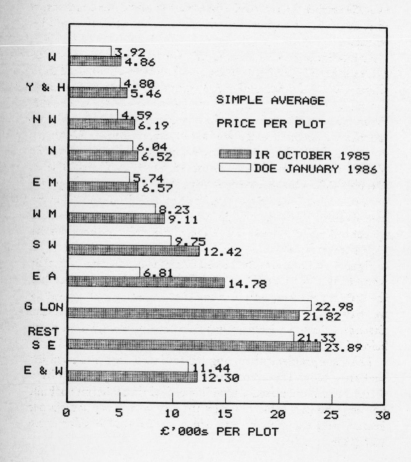

We are drawn to the conclusion, therefore, that the data in the *Property Market Report* is more appropriate than the DoE's for use in calculating the residential land value of Britain. It does not include Scotland, but neither does the DoE's. Bulk land alone will be used, because the proportionate contribution of other sites is not known. This must lead to considerable under-estimation, but if mid-1985 rather than late-1985 figures are required (for comparison with the national income, say) then the under-estimation will be reduced.

An interesting sidelight on the difference between the two sets of figures is provided by Vallis's research for the 1960s, referred to in Appendix 1. Vallis found the median transaction price per hectare for residential land in England in the mid-1960s to be £24,463. From 1969 to 1971 such prices in England and Wales were almost identical to simple average prices per hectare (Evans 1974: xvii). Applying the DoE's private sector housing land price index to Vallis's figure raises it by almost 18 times to £437,000/ha in October 1985. One would expect this result to be on the large side for two reasons — it is not restricted to bulk land, and it hugely over-represents London and the South East. Nevertheless it would appear to support the use of the Inland Revenue's rather than the DoE's set of figures.

Figure 6: II compares the Inland Revenue information with that from the DoE for 1986 (DoE 1987: Table 10.1). It can be seen that the only major divergence between the two sets is over the values for East Anglia (the smallest region), which suggests that the District Valuers spotted the incipient land price explosion there before it actually registered in the prices of transactions.

The main problem with using the IR data is that it is given for land areas only. The average prices per plot in Figure 6: II have therefore been calculated by dividing the values per hectare of bulk housing land (see Table 7: IV) by the average number of plots per hectare in the transactions recorded in the DoE/SDD/WO's Table 10.1 (1986: 105-107).

Local Authority Housing

There is no source of information which enables us to value the land under local authority dwellings. In any case the land is not available on the open market under free market conditions and the constraints on its use would be expected to lower its value. There would therefore seem to be little point in attempting to obtain official valuations even if they were recorded by local authorities. Local authority land held for future house building would also be recorded at values which would be uninformative.

There are exceptions to the low esteem in which council house property is often held. In London there are opportunities for capitalising on the land price boom which have given considerable windfall gains. In Battersea and Chelsea even high rise flats have taken on a new lease of life and have become desirable properties with attractive views across the Thames and the City. Record figures have been achieved in very short times. On September 23, 1987, the London *Evening News* reported the case of a 77-year-old pensioner who bought his 6-bedroom semi in Purley for £22,000 in June 1986 and sold it nine months later for £105,000. More typically a 3-bedroom semi bought in 1981 sold for £75,000 six years later. An apartment with a good view could sell for £130,000. These properties are here recorded in the private ownership category and carry the average land value estimates used in our calculations.

In *Regional Trends* (1987) Tables 3.1 and 3.4 give the total stock of dwellings and the breakdown by tenure, 'owner occupied', 'rented/local authority' and 'rented/other'. In the case of 'rented/other' with no information to the contrary, site values have been taken as the average for the region. However, in the case of 'rented/local authority' we can make an adjustment related to density of dwellings. DoE/SDD/WO (1986 : 86) gives the average number of dwellings per hectare for tenders accepted as 45.8 in England and Wales, with small variations between the regions. The figures used in Tables 6 : I and 6 : II show that the 1,125 hectares bought with housing planning permission represented 26,839 plots, giving 23.8 dwellings per hectare. On a rough deduction it is not unreasonable to take local authority housing plots at half the value of privately owned plots. This could also be considered as a compromise position encompassing both council houses in very undesirable areas and new land purchases for which higher prices will have to be paid. Some local authorities, for example, have given high rise blocks of flats to property developers for nothing in return for refurbishment of other properties retained in local authority control; whilst on the other hand council house building has been priced out of contention because of high land prices. The land cost per hectare of tenders accepted by local authorities in England and Wales in 1985 was higher than the equivalent private sector cost (DoE/SDD/WO : 82, 88, 107).

Total Value of Residential Land

Table 6 : III gives for the total number of dwellings in each region or country the percentage split in ownership as stated in *Regional Trends* (1987 : Table 3.4). In calculating the land value we have taken the IR figure for each region or country as given in Figure 6 : II for owner occupied dwellings and 'rented other'. In the case of local authority rented dwellings we have taken the 50% figure as explained above.

This gives a total figure for Great Britain of £239.6bn, of which £28.9bn is attributed to local authority residential land.

Our final estimate is for land already purchased for the purpose of dwellings. Large property development companies carry large land banks; even smaller companies are interested in buying land as far ahead as their financial resources will allow in order to profit by the steady rise in land values. For this reason it is very difficult to estimate how much land is held for this purpose at any given time. Whilst the amount of land purchased in England and Wales for dwellings in the private sector was recorded as an average of 2,387 hectares from 1981 to 1985 representing 56,800 plots, the number of houses completed was twice this figure, averaging 134,500 from 1983 to 1985. About a tenth of the amount of land was purchased for the public sector and the number of dwellings completed has declined steeply from 98,500 in 1980 in England and Wales to 35,200 in 1985. We have therefore taken an arbitrary figure equivalent to the sum of purchases made in the last three years, in this way making some allowance for the stocks of land which have

Table 6 : III
Regional and national residential land value aggregates

Region or country	Stock of dwellings			Total housing land values (£ bn)	Local authority share (£ bn)
	% owner occupied	% rented l.a.	% rented other		
North	55	34	11	6.70	0.11
Yorks. and Humberside	62	29	10	9.08	1.32
East Midlands	66	24	10	8.89	1.07
East Anglia	66	22	13	10.47	1.15
Greater London	55	29	17	52.33	7.59
Rest of S. East	70	20	10	87.39	8.74
South West	69	18	12	20.62	1.86
West Midlands	63	28	9	15.70	2.20
North West	65	26	9	13.56	1.76
Wales	67	23	10	4.81	0.55
Scotland	41	50	9	10.00*	2.50
Great Britain				239.55	28.85

Formula used for calculation per region and per country:

(Privately owned % + rented other % + 0.5 rented l.a. %) × stock of dwellings (Table 6 : I) × average plot price (Figure 6 : II).

* Assumes an average plot price in Scotland as in the North.

been held for longer periods. The figure used is almost certain to be an underestimate. CSO statistics give us the number of hectares purchased for England and Wales in the private sector and the number of *transactions* in the public sector. The purchases in 1983 to 1985 in the private sector add up to 8,007 hectares; adding a tenth for the public sector gives 8,800 hectares. To allow for Scotland in order to arrive at a Great Britain figure requires the figure to be increased in proportion to the number of houses completed, i.e. 168.4 to 186.7, giving a final figure of 9,756 hectares.

At the GB average price per hectare for private sector land of £277,000 per hectare we arrive at a land value of £2.7bn.

Adding this figure to that arrived at above gives us a total of £242.3bn. Even though the number of houses under construction is considered well below that required to meet our needs it is in excess of the amount of land currently being purchased for future dwellings. It is not surprising that since 1985 land values have been escalating rapidly.

This figure does not include vacant land which may be used for housing. For our present purposes it is sufficient to refer to Table 8 : IX in Chapter 8, and add 6.7bn, raising the grand total capital value of GB residential land to £249bn.

A Check by the Spatial Method

The IR data may be used directly to provide a semi-independent check of the total arrived at via plot numbers. Multiplying the average price per hectare — £277,000 assuming Scottish prices were the same as those in the Northern region, and weighting them in proportion to housing stock — by the area of housing land calculated in Chapter 4 — 920,000ha — produces an aggregate value of £254.8bn. This figure includes vacant land that was once used for housing, and so is directly comparable with the figure of £249bn above. There is no need to calculate the area of residential land occupied by local authority dwellings as its value per hectare — not per plot — has been taken to be roughly the same as for private land.

National Wealth Estimates: A Check by the Residual Method

The CSO's estimates of National Wealth (Bryant 1987) give Personal Sector Wealth for 1985 as £1,165bn, residential buildings comprising £527.8bn of this. However, after including the intangible value of private sector housing tenant rights the total of privately owned land and buildings becomes £563.7bn.

The CSO capital stock estimates of replacement cost based on the perpetual inventory method (reliability given as less than 80%)

give a total value of privately owned housing buildings as £376.8bn. The land value is supposedly obtained by difference:

> 563.7
> 376.8
> ─────
> £186.9bn i.e. 33.1% of gross value
> ─────

If the gross capital stock estimate is 10% too high, which would not be unlikely (see Chapter 8), then the land value becomes £221bn, compared with the equivalent figure of £211bn in Table 6:III, which excludes Northern Ireland.

The figure for all residential buildings in the National Balance Sheet including tenants' interests is made up as follows:

Personal sector	556.1
Industrial and commercial	7.6
Central government	1.7
Local authorities	127
Public corporations	2.7
	£695bn

The CSO's private land-to-buildings ratio of 1-to-3 gives a land value of £232bn. M. C. Flemming (1986 : 313), in his authoritative survey of statistical sources, comments on the figures in the National Balance Sheet (before they were somewhat improved — Bryant 1987 : 113): '... the estimates are again open to very wide margins of error. The land and buildings elements in particular are regarded as the least reliable parts and indeed have been referred to as being "rather shaky" (Pettigrew, 1980, pp. 97 and 99). In general the figures should be regarded as providing no more than indicators of broad order of magnitude.' Nevertheless, this alternative method, which is equivalent to the test applied in Chapter 8 for commercial and industrial land, and considering the likely over-statement of replacement costs, certainly indicates that our figure of £249bn must be 'in the right ball park!'

7

Commercial and Industrial Land

JOHN LOVELESS

THE OBJECTIVE estimation of land values is possible only where there are numerous transactions from which mean values may be derived. The value of agricultural and residential land can thus be estimated with a high degree of accuracy because of the frequent sales among these categories of land use. In contrast, accuracy is harder to obtain with industrial land and very difficult to achieve (at the present time) with commercial land because relatively few transactions occur in these categories of land use. Furthermore, it seems that the details of the small number of transactions involving commercial land, which regularly appear in property magazines, have *only once* been collated. This research, by Vallis (1972), assessed the changes in land value in Britain over a period of nearly 80 years, for three categories of urban land use, namely residential, industrial and commercial.

The present estimates are a collation of all the available information on the value of commercial and industrial land in Britain. All the data have been corrected to equivalent values as at the end of 1985. The final valuation was derived in the following way.

First, the total area of developed land in Britain was estimated (see Chapter 4); this was then divided into regional areas. The

Table 7 : I
The total value of industrial and commercial land in Great Britain as at 31st December, 1985

Commercial land	£107.7 billion
Industrial land	£35.5 billion

percentage area of urban land in each region dedicated to a particular land use was next estimated. Finally, a mean value for industrial and commercial land in each region was derived, and regional totals for each use calculated. These were then aggregated and found to be as shown in Table 7 : I.

The Total Area of Urban Land

The total area of urban land in Britain is a fairly well established figure. Researchers have made estimates which are presented in Chapter 4. A 1985 figure of 1.78m ha (4.4m acres) for England and Wales and 2.02m ha (5m acres) for Great Britain was established.

Land value and the percentage of land in urban use varies considerably from one region to another. Any tolerably accurate estimate of the total value must therefore allow for these divisions. In Table 7 : II, data for the percentage of land which is in urban use in each economic planning region has been summarised from Best's

Table 7 : II
The regional distribution of urban land in Britain

Region	Total area ('000 ha)	Percentage urban 1960	1970	1985	Urban area* ('000 ha)
SE	2,740	15	19	20	550
SW	2,370	7	8	8	190
EA	1,240	5	7	7	85
EM	1,270	9	11	11	145
WM	1,300	12	13	13	170
Y&H	1,420	11	12	12	170
NW	750	23	26	26	195
N	1,940	6	7	7	135
W	2,080	4	7	7	145
S	7,720	3	3	3	240
Total	22,830	(7)	(8)	9	2025

* Extrapolated values, referring to the economic planning regions as they were in 1971.

tabulation of the results of three surveys (Best 1981 : 65). These surveys were carried out in the 1960s so some extrapolation is necessary to update their findings to 1985. A particular difficulty here could be in allowing for the population drift to the South East. In the event, the order of extrapolation required to update the figure was very small.

The importance of making the calculations at the regional level may be gauged from the evidence that the South East accounts for 58% of the total residential land value of Britain (Table 6 : III). To obtain the most accurate figure for the total land value, effort should be concentrated in the regions having the greatest relative land value.

Commercial and Industrial Land Area

An attempt was made in Chapter 4 to determine the area of the nation's land which is actually dedicated to commercial and industrial uses. It is particularly important to obtain an accurate figure for the percentage area of commercial land, the value of which can be over twenty times as great as those in other uses. Unfortunately very few of the existing studies separate out commercial land as a discrete statistic.

In the Second Land Utilisation Survey, commercial land was included with residential land and the two together comprised, in total, 48% of the urban area! We calculate that commercial land amounted to about 2.25% of the urban area in 1985.

For the regional variation it is assumed that the degree of commercialisation in any area is related to the percentage of the rates paid by commerce. Table 7 : III shows the percentage of the rates paid by commerce and industry in the standard economic regions of England and Wales. Inner London and Leeds have been picked out to verify that it is the cities which raise the national average, and the towns, villages and rural transport routes (included in the urban definition) which lower it. The average for England and Wales is greater than the average for each of the regions, testifying to the national importance of the Inner London boroughs. Detailed studies of these boroughs are needed to provide information on the extent and value of commercial land.

Table 7 : III
Percentage of the rates paid by commerce and industry in various regions

Region	% commercial	% industrial
Inner London	55	2
Outer London	24	11
Rest SE	22	10
SW	22	8
EA	22	11
EM	21	14
WM	20	14
Y&H	21	13
(Leeds)	(29)	(11)
NW	22	12
(Merseyside)	(21)	(12)
N	18	14
W	18	14
England and Wales	27	10

Source: Municipal Year Book, 1986.

To illustrate this importance one has only to consider the distribution of commercial offices. According to an Inland Revenue Valuation Office survey for the end of 1985 (IRVO no. 47 : 45), the Cities of London and Westminster alone account for 48% of the capital value of all the offices in England and Wales, the rest of London accounts for another 26% and the rest of the South East another 10%.

Industrial Land Values

The final problem was to determine the mean value of industrial and commercial land in each region. The more straightforward of these was the estimation of industrial land value. Five data sets (Vallis 1972, IRVO 46 & 47, Fothergill 1985, *The Estates Gazette* 17 February 1987) were compared in order to arrive at the final figures

Table 7 : IV
Industrial land values at the end of 1985
(£'000/ha)

Region	IRVO no. 46	Fothergill	The Estates Gazette	Final	Housing land values*
London	990	1,070	—	990	1,200
Rest SE	690	610	690	670	547
SW	270	290	350	280	287
EA	210	180	230	210	272
EM	150	180	160	160	161
WM	200	200	190	200	205
Y&H	200	150	160	170	142
NW	150	150	140	150	143
N	70	70	70	70	150
W	100	90	—	100	102
S	—	—	110	110	150

* See page 97.

shown in Table 7 : IV. All the figures were corrected to equivalent values for the end of 1985 using the Retail Price Index. Among the five data sets two are not shown in Table 7 : IV. The values obtained by Vallis were considered to be out of date and the other set, which were for the Enterprise Zones only, were considered unrepresentative. Nevertheless, both of these, in general, confirmed the values of the other data sets.

An interesting fact emerges from a comparison of Vallis's figures for the late 1960s with the latest data. Land values in Wales have suffered a relative decline, while those in the South West have advanced significantly. This was not the intention of politicians who sanctioned the construction of the M4 and the Severn Bridge! The idea was that South Wales would benefit from improved access to London.

It is also interesting to note, in passing, that the values for industrial land shown in Table 7 : IV are not dissimilar to those shown in Chapter 6 for residential land.

Commercial Land Values

The estimation of commercial land value is more difficult. Vallis (1972), for example, looking at median price levels, suggested that for England as a whole, commercial land values were 22 times residential values and 20 times industrial values in the mid-1960s. But the commercial land sampled was mainly in central London, so the comparison appears actually to have been rather one between the city centre and the suburbs (see Appendix 1). Since that time it appears that residential land value, instead of remaining a little lower than industrial, has become slightly greater. This may indicate that the continuing extension of the green belts around Britain's cities is forcing up residential land values in general and not just in the South East region as is commonly supposed.

The only thoroughgoing survey of urban land values in Britain, which was carried out for the town of Whitstable in 1973 by Wilks, revealed that the street value of the main commercial centre was about ten times the average residential street value. However, Wilks noted several reasons why shop values in Whitstable were depressed at that time, and also the fact that house values had surged by 25% in the previous nine months (The Land Institute 1974:8-9). In any event, Whitstable can hardly rate as an important centre of commerce with a population of only 25,000.

For Bristol in 1985 a valuer with extensive local knowledge estimated the value of city centre commercial land at about 20 times the general industrial level and 12.5 times the general residential level. A clear pattern, therefore, emerges regarding the general relationship between central and suburban land values. The problem lies in finding a general relationship between the *average* level of commercial land values and average industrial and residential values so that the latter, which are relatively well known, may be used to calculate the former.

An impressionistic approach, backed up by the observations in Appendix 1, is the quickest way forward. Let us assign the nation's commercial land to three categories, occupying say 10%, 50% and 40% respectively of the commercial area. First, there are the prime areas of the major centres serving whole regions or sub-regions. Then there are the surrounds of the prime areas and all the secondary commercial centres serving districts. Finally, there is all the distributed commercial property having no real focal point. If these categories are valued at 25, 10 and 2.5 times the industrial/residential value the net multiplier is 8.5. In reality there is a full spectrum of values spreading from around the residential value upwards to about 200 times that value in the City of London. Nevertheless, this model may be conceptually useful.

For any individual site a key determinant of its value will be existing use rights, as defined by the appropriate planning permission. These rights usually remain forever since, once granted, they are the rightful property of the owner just as much as the bricks and

Table 7 : V
The value of commercial land in Britain
at the end of 1985

Region	Urban area[1] ('000 ha)	% commercial	Land value (£M/ha)	Gross value (£ billion)
City of London	0.27	40.0	106.0	11.45
Westminster	2.2	15.0	33.3	10.99
Rest of London	137	3.7	4.29	21.75
Rest of SE	405	2.2	3.83	34.13
SW	195	2.2	1.62	6.95
EA	90	2.2	1.22	2.42
EM	150	2.1	0.93	2.93
WM	170	2.0	1.16	3.94
Y&H	170	2.1	0.99	3.53
NW	190	2.2	0.87	3.64
N	130	1.9	0.41	1.01
W	145	1.9	0.58	1.60
S	240	2.2	0.64	3.38
Total	2,025	2.25	2.36	107.72

1. Adjustments have been made to the urban areas of the pre-1974 economic planning regions as set out in Table 7:II to make them apply to the present planning regions.

Table 7 : VI
The value of industrial land[1] in Britain at the end of 1985

Region	Urban area[2] ('000 ha)	% industrial[1]	Land value (£'000/ha)	Gross value (£ billion)
SE	545	4.2	840	19.2
SW	195	4.6	280	2.5
EA	90	6.2	210	1.2
EM	150	8.1	160	1.9
WM	170	8.1	200	2.8
Y&H	170	7.7	170	2.2
NW	190	6.9	150	2.0
N	130	8.1	70	0.7
W	145	8.1	100	1.2
S	240	6.3	110	1.7
Total	2,025	6.3	278	35.5

1. Industrial includes utilities.
2. See note 1, Table 7:V.

mortar. The value of each site is no doubt affected by many other variables. Nevertheless, it is still possible to postulate a mean value. If the mean value of industrial land in Britain at the end of 1985 was £278,000/ha (Table 7 : VI), then the mean value of commercial land becomes £2.36m/ha.

Regional Analysis of Industry and Commerce

To estimate the area of land in each region which is in commercial or industrial use reference has been made to the data derived in Table 7 : III. This shows the percentage of the rates in each region which is paid by commerce and industry. By comparing the regional figures with the national figures the relative commercialisation and industrialisation of each region may be determined and we would expect this to be reflected in land utilisation.

The factor of 8.5 for converting industrial to commercial values applies to the nation as a whole, so it has been adjusted when applied to the regions to take account of the fact that the commercial land values for the Cities of London and Westminster have been calculated separately and are a disproportionate share of the total (see Appendix 1). The factor for all the regions has to be reduced to 5.8 to be consistent with the national factor of 8.5.

The total value of commercial land in Britain was found to be £107.7bn, 21% of which was in the City and Westminster (Table 7 : V). The total value of industrial land was found to be £35.5bn (Table 7 : VI).

8

The Spatial Methodology: A Test

DAVID RICHARDS

THE SPATIAL method was adopted for this study because it is the most direct approach to calculating the value of land. The reliability of this method of assessment was tested against the results produced by the residual method, which is used by valuers and property developers. We selected industrial and commercial land for this part of our investigation because it is the sector with the least precise land value estimates. The spatial method concluded that commercial and industrial land was worth about £143 bn in 1985 (Chapter 7), and the residual method produced a figure of £135 bn.

For reasons given below, we believe the spatial method of assessment is the more reliable and offers the greater potential for further refinement for the purposes of constructing an inventory of the value of the nation's land in its various uses.

The arithmetic of the residual method is as follows. Multiply the floorspace of commercial and industrial properties by their rental values. Apply the appropriate yields (years purchase) to convert the rents to capital values. From the capital values subtract the net replacement costs of the buildings to leave the properties' residual land values. The data sources are the rating authorities' floorspace returns (DoE 1986a; Welsh Office 1986), professional opinions of the general level of rents and yields for each type of property, and the net capital stock estimates of the National Accounts, supplemented by the Royal Institution of Chartered Surveyors' guidelines on building costs (BCIS February 1986).

An immediate problem with this approach is that it assumes that all properties are developed to their full potential. Any property which is not must yield an annual rent which depresses its capitalised value, and hence (despite the lower net replacement cost) its residual land value. But, as asset strippers know, land value cannot be depressed in this way. Its open market value depends on the best alternative permitted use of the land, not its current use. At the extreme, vacant land, which probably accounts for over 5% of the urban area of Britain, has no value at all according to this methodology. One would therefore expect aggregate land value to be considerably under-estimated.

Land Values in the UK Balance Sheet

The CSO's modest attempt to calculate the capital value of UK land involved the subtraction of capital (buildings) stock estimates for the major sectors of the economy, which appear in the Blue Book, from its balance sheet estimates of the market value of buildings and civil engineering works. The former represent the replacement cost of buildings, the latter include the land the buildings stand on, valued at current use. The construction industry's land banks were included, but the 100,000 or more hectares of vacant urban land were not.

Bryant noted the major methodological weaknesses of the exercise: 'First capital stock estimates are extremely dependent on assumptions about asset lives which must often be rough. Secondly the question arises whether comparison should be made between market values of land and buildings in the balance sheets and gross capital stock or net (i.e. depreciated) capital stock' (Bryant 1987 : 100).

The CSO elected to use gross capital stock for housing, where depreciation does not appear to be very significant, 'at least not until the older dwellings are nearing the end of their useful life.' Even so this would tend to overstate the buildings component of the housing stock. Five per cent of it is 'unfit for habitation' and 15% is over 100 years old. Given that older houses tend to be in higher value locations, it would not seem unreasonable to suggest that most of the value of, say, a fifth of the housing stock resides in the land occupied, and that subtracting the costs to replace the buildings anew almost wipes out that land value.

For commercial and industrial properties, where depreciation is important, the CSO chose to use net figures. Bryant cited the College of Estate Management's 1986 report *Depreciation of Commercial Property* as indicating heavy depreciation of capital values in the first 10 years of the life of such properties: 'They suggest for example that 20 year old office blocks may be worth only one-third of the value of similar brand new buildings. This includes site values which, if excluded, would reduce the value of some 20-year-old office blocks to close to zero.' Bryant added that market commentators believe that property values have been particularly affected since 1980 because 'technological changes have changed tenants' requirements faster and the impact of depreciation is likely to be greater when the property market is weak.'

In view of these developments it is noteworthy that the net capital stock estimates in the Blue Book are arrived at by straight-line depreciation assuming 80-year asset lives for commercial buildings and 60-year lives for industrial buildings built since 1930 (CSO 1985 : 201). They must, therefore, overstate the value of the buildings. The structure of the obsolete 20-year-old office block would be recorded in the national accounts as worth three-quarters of its real original cost when in fact it has virtually no economic value at all. The whole of that over-estimate would then be subtracted from the site value which would become a negative quantity.

The CSO did not publish its land calculations for public sector residential and other buildings, but noted that its balance sheet valuation of the former barely covered the Blue Book building stock, and that the latter exhibited lower land values than in the private sector. It is even clearer here, therefore, that the methodology loses much of what it is supposed to measure. The land value of the public sector must be a substantial proportion of the total. Publicly-owned land was estimated by Dowrick (1974) as covering almost 16% of the area of Britain. We estimate publicly-owned land as constituting about 45% of urban land (Chapter 4). The government spent 45% of the nation's gross domestic product (at market prices) in 1985. It is inconceivable that all the land occupied by the public sector should have a negative value, as implied by the CSO study.

The problem is partly one of definition. Bryant stated that 'In the case of non-residential buildings the lower land values in the public sector than in the private sector reflect Valuation Office advice that land values for community assets are much lower than values for housing and commercial use' (1987:101). This advice once again amounts to a current use definition of land value rather than the true economic definition which is the land's value in its highest permitted alternative use (its 'opportunity cost'). If government wishes to assess the efficiency to which land under its control is put, then that is the value which it should put on its holdings.

In the case of residential buildings Bryant commented that 'it would appear that the cost of construction . . . is not reflected in the values which these buildings might fetch on the open market.' In fact, it is probably the value of the land which has been lost. But there is a conceptual problem here. The site value of any individual house on a council estate is clearly reduced by its presence within the estate. However, were the whole estate to be sold to its tenants it is likely that the 'magic of ownership' would transform land values. So the question arises: to what extent does the opportunity cost principle apply to whole areas as opposed to individual sites? Does 27% of the housing stock of the nation occupy land of negative economic value? Do not the vast council estates near the centres of our cities occupy some of the prime sites of Britain?

Additionally, the points made above with regard to the depreciation of buildings apply forcibly to local authority dwellings, especially of the high rise variety.

CSO Data: The Statistical Accuracy

The foregoing are reasons for arguing that the CSO has underestimated the value of UK land. But the unadjusted estimate itself is also fairly imprecise. The CSO makes an assessment of the quality of its statistics and those involved in the land value calculation are among the poorest that they publish. The national accounts data gathering process means that 'It is not possible to calculate statistical margins of error in a scientific way' (CSO 1985: 21). However, a subjective judgment is made of the range within which estimates have roughly a 90% chance of being correct. For both the balance sheet and the capital stock estimates the three

grades generally used have to be extended by the addition of a
fourth, D, 'used for errors of more than 20%' (CSO 1985 : 201).

Taking the balance sheet first, the estimate for the tangible assets
of the UK as a whole, 75% of which is buildings and works, is
believed to be 'in the range of ±3% to 10%, i.e. grade B (Bryant
1987 : 94). This means that there may be about a 10% chance that
the tangible assets of the UK in 1985, put at £1,444.5bn, were either
more than £1,589bn or less than £1,300bn.

Individual components are generally less reliably estimated than
aggregates. The figure for the tangible assets of industrial and
commercial companies has a D rating. The financial sector's tangible assets are more accurately assessed, but they are only worth
one-fifth as much. It is not surprising that this sector should be
ranked alongside local authorities as the least accurately assessed.
According to Bryant, 'the value of land and buildings owned by
industrial and commercial companies had to be obtained as a
residual of estimates for all the other sectors' (1987 : 101).

The same problem afflicts land values: they are estimated as
residuals. And the second set of data used in their calculation
appears to be as unreliable as the first. The gross capital stock
estimates of the Blue Book are thought to be mostly of grade C
quality, 'but some of them are much less reliable than others.' The
capital consumption figures used to obtain from these the net
figures are regarded as having the same margin of error (i.e. a 90%
probability of being correct within a range of ±10-20%).

Given these accuracies, and adopting the narrowest possible
ranges of reliability, the CSO's land value calculations may be set
out as in Table 8 : I.

Land Values in the CSO/District Valuer's Survey

The method by which the balance sheet market values were
obtained may be used to check part of Table 8 : I. The Inland
Revenue Valuation Office was commissioned to carry out a sample
survey of 2,600 commercial and industrial properties in England
and Wales. For each property in the sample District Valuers were
asked to record its 1973 rateable value and its 31 December 1985
gross rental value, capital value and existing use site value. The

Table 8 : I
CSO estimate of UK non-agricultural, non-mineral, non-waste, existing use land value (end-1985, £bn)

Sector	Estimate	Approx. confidence limits 90%	99.5%
(A) Private sector residential			
Buildings and land	563.7	547-581	
Buildings only	376.8	365-388	
Implied land value	186.9		159-216
(B) Other private sector buildings and civil engineering works			
Buildings and land	237.8	190-285	
Buildings only	153.7	131-177	
Implied land value	84.6		13-154
(C) Public sector residential and other buildings and works	Either negligible or imponderable		
(D) Total land value (with approx. 99.9% confidence limits)	271.5		(172-370)

average ratio of end-1985 capital value to rateable value for the observations in each class of hereditament was then applied to each class's rateable value (1973 rental value) to produce its end-1985 capital value. The results were summarised in the *Property Market Report, (PMR)* No. 44 for Spring 1987, and the aggregate findings are presented in Table 8 : II.

For the sake of comparison with section (B) of Table 8 : I the differences of coverage must be noted. Table 8 : II does not include Scotland and Northern Ireland, nor certain types of property, principally North Sea oil and gas installations and the properties of non profit making bodies. The inclusion of the first might be expected to lower the overall ratio of land value to property value slightly, as northern regions have lower than average ratios. The second might also be expected to lower the ratio slightly, as it has

Table 8 : II
Valuation Office estimate of the value of
industrial and commercial properties in England and Wales
(end-1985, £bn)

Asset	Estimate	Approx. 90% confidence limits
Buildings and land	173	167-179
Existing use site values	54	43-65
Implied building values	119	107-131

no land element at all. The effect of the third should be neutral as the survey found little variation in ratios between different types of buildings. Table 8:II, therefore, suggests a land to property value ratio for GB of perhaps 29%, whereas Table 8:I, section (B), has a ratio of around 36%.

This result is rather surprising. As the figures for land and buildings are linked the difference in ratios must be due either to under-valuation of sites by District Valuers or under-valuation of the building stock by the CSO. If the earlier argument is correct, the CSO has actually over-valued buildings, so the conclusion would seem to be that the District Valuers under-valued sites considerably. Alternatively, the wide margins of error in both statistical exercises may have been to blame.

Further enquiry of the CSO has revealed that the site value question in the DV survey was indeed the one that posed the most problems. Framing it was difficult, so a straightforward question was put, leaving the District Valuers to interpret it. The consistency of the replies was not investigated, but in view of the findings of the College of Estate Management the degree of uniformity in the site value percentages came as a surprise. It may have been that the buildings component of properties was sometimes over-valued due to the lack of site transactions available for comparison. Direct market evidence of site values is scarce compared with that for developed properties, so we would expect the site value question to be the least accurately answered. The CSO itself does not accord a high degree of reliability to the site value aggregate, which it puts at 'D', as opposed to 'B' for the overall valuation of land and buildings. Random sampling of the rating valuation lists was not possible because of the way they are framed, so confidence limits could not be estimated. The rough accuracy gradings are applied in Table 8 : II with the narrowest possible margins of error (i.e. 3% for grade B, 10% for C and 20% for D).

Further very broad checks may be made on certain aspects of the problem. First, the balance sheet estimates. Taken in conjunction with floorspace data these imply rental levels for different types of property. *PMR 44* listed the average yields for the classes of property surveyed. These are applied in Table 8 : III to the total capital values of those classes to find their total gross rental values (landlords having responsibility for repairs and insurance). The floorspace areas of those classes (DOE 1986a, Welsh Office 1986) are then used to ascertain the implied average gross rents per square metre for each class.

The *PMR* classes had to be harmonised with the floorspace classes. Restaurants were taken as 0.134 of 'Hotels, Restaurants and Public Houses' as that was their proportion of that class's rateable value in 1985. Hotels, public houses and 'other commercial and industrial buildings' had to be omitted from the calculations as their areas are not published. Neither does the floorspace data include certain mainly large-scale manufacturing establishments, such as iron and steel works and refineries, for which floorspace measurements are inappropriate. However, rateable plant and equipment, which forms the bulk of the value of such properties, and about one-tenth of the industrial total according to Bryant, has been excluded from the figures.

Housing had to be treated separately. Its total capital value, including tenants' 'intangible' interests, had to be deduced from the tables in the balance sheets. The average yield was assumed to be 8%, on the advice of those surveyors who could be prevailed upon to make educated guesses despite the lack of market evidence. The floorspace area was calculated by multiplying the number of rateable hereditaments by 70 square metres. This was taken as a conservative average of the representative dwellings described in the appendixes of the *PMR*. It also represents the average floor area of new council houses in the mid-1970s (DoE/SDD/WO 1986 : 82). Finally, it was decided to work with the UK figures rather than attempt to deduct estimates for Scotland and N. Ireland, which anyway would not lower the final outcome by more than 2%.

Table 8 : III indicates a clear rent structure. It is perhaps surprising that dwellings precisely bisect commerce and industry, which is no doubt a testimony to their vastly superior tax position.

Table 8 : III
Valuation Office estimates of gross rental values of property classes in England and Wales (late 1985)

Class	Total gross rent (£bn)	Floorspace (million metres^2)	Gross rent per metre^2
Commercial offices	3.45	50.81	67.9
Shops and restaurants	4.20	81.25	51.7
Warehouses and open storage	2.47	160.53	15.4
Industry	2.65	232.22	11.4
Dwellings (UK)	55.50	1,540.00	36.0

The Residual Method: Retail Property

The levels at which the rents are pitched in Table 8:III, however, cannot be independently checked until further work has been done on the property market as a whole. Research is needed

1   on the distribution of rental values from the prime sites to the marginal sites, and

2   on the distribution of floorspace along the rental gradients between the prime and the marginal sites.

Existing data, such as in the *Property Market Reports,* relates only to the investment property markets, not the rump of tertiary shops and old industrial sheds. Peak rents are the focus of attention and generalised rent assessments are limited to prime areas and the best secondary areas. Shops in Newcastle, for example, are the subject of a special article in *PMR 44*, but heroic assumptions are necessary to convert the exceptional detail made available in that article into figures to compare with Table 8 : III. The article, 'Focus on Retailing in Newcastle', by the District Valuer, provides the following information. The 1985 peak was £1,300/m^2 Zone A. City centre rents graded down to about £300/m^2. Secondary centres commanded about £100-200/m^2. The City centre contained 1,075 shopping units and 375,000m^2, and the fringes and suburbs 'more than 2,000 units' (2,500, occupying 430,300m^2 by deduction from DoE 1986a : 30).

What we do not know is how the Zone A rents relate to the average rents for the whole floor areas of the shops, the distribution of floorspace and rents within the City centre and within the outer area, and how representative Newcastle as a whole is of the whole of the Northern Region. We must hazard some guesses.

The average shop size in the City centre was about 350m^2. Such a shop with a 10m frontage would have an average floorspace value of about one-third the Zone A value if the standard procedure of 'halving back' the rent every 6.1m and zero rating a small staff/ storage area is applied. Outside the centre, the average floor area was about 170m^2 and halving back, assuming a 6.1m frontage, produces an average rent per square metre of just less than half the Zone A rent. The suburbs of Newcastle may in fact be fairly representative of England and Wales as a whole in which the average shop size is 137m^2. 140m^2 is the size used in the Investor's Chronicle/Hillier Parker shop rent index.

On this basis, and taking £500 as the average Zone A rent for the City centre, the overall average central rent may have been £165/m^2. As for the suburbs, we are not told how low the shop rents reached. But we may assume that they would not have fallen below housing levels, which at three-quarters of the national average, would have been about £25/m^2. Overall suburban rents must therefore have varied from about £100/m^2 to £25/m^2, with a straight average of about £65/m^2. The average, weighted by floorspace, for Newcastle becomes £109, or about one-quarter of the peak level.

We are still in the dark as to the levels of shop rents outside

Newcastle. There were about 4.2m m^2 of floorspace in the rest of the Northern Region. If we take the average for outer Newcastle as representative, the average for the region becomes £68/m^2.

There are two ways of extending this benchmark analysis to the rest of the nation. First, by assuming that the relationship between aggregate shop rental income and aggregate personal disposable income in the North (the former was 2.8% of the latter) held good for all the other standard economic regions. Second, as a check, by assuming that the relationship between prime shop rents and the average in the North (the latter being about 14.5% of the former — 'prime levels', not the peak rent) also held good for all the regions.

Table 8 : IV takes 2.8% of the personal disposable income in each region (from *Regional Trends 22* 1987: 128) and divides it by the amount of retail floorspace to estimate the region's average shop rent. This is compared with 14.5% of the prime regional rent. The former is a much more dependable statistic than the latter. It is based on an exhaustive database, whereas the latter depends on impressionistic evidence gleaned from *PMR 44*. In compiling the latter, exceptional peaks in Newcastle, Edinburgh, Liverpool and Cardiff have been rounded down to £1,000/m^2 Zone A, which it is believed was more comparable with the 'prime levels' figure given for most other centres. Another problem was choosing a representative shop shape and size for converting Zone A rents into overall rents. For this purpose the 140m^2 (6.1m by 18.3m plus 28m^2 of staff/storage area) of the Investor's Chronicle/Hillier Parker shop rent index was chosen. This accounts for the low average/prime ratio for the Northern Region used in calculating this rent statistic.

This statistic does, however, pick up one important regional circumstance which should not be overlooked. Shops in Central London are uniquely dependent on tourists, whether of the foreign or the home-grown variety. Their rental levels would be expected to exceed those predicted by indigenous disposable income alone. The prime rents in Oxford Street in 1985 were around the £1,850/m^2 Zone A mark. It is difficult to translate that into overall rents per square metre, but at a factor of one-half the 14.5% equivalent would be more than double the national average. For Central London (2,528m m^2), therefore, the aggregate rent has been doubled in finding the national total (Table 8 : IV, column 1).

Table 8 : IV
**Two estimates of average retail rental levels
in the standard economic regions of Britain in 1985**

Region	(1) 2.8% of personal disposable income (£m)	(2) Retail floorspace (million m²)	(3) Average retail rent (£/m²)	(4) 14.5% of prime rents (£/m²)
North	338.6	4.982	68.0	68
North West	728.5	10.674	68.2	68
Yorks. and Humber.	538.6	7.657	70.3	56
East Midlands	443.6	5.946	74.6	34
West Midlands	580.0	7.859	73.8	63
East Anglia	233.5	3.210	72.7	58
South West	523.2	7.694	68.0	48
Greater London	988.5	13.674	72.3	59-161
South East (rest)	1286.2	15.162	84.8	68
Wales	297.5	4.397	68.0	68
Scotland	601.3	8.843*	68.0	87
Great Britain	6,926 (see text)	90.1	76.9 (see text)	

* Assumed

Factories and Warehouses

Turning to industry and warehousing the same problem confronts us: how do we convert the available data on the better quality properties into averages for all properties? The *Property Market Reports* provide us with an extensive coverage of non-High Tech buildings erected within the previous ten years, divided into five categories. Their yields correspond approximately with the *PMR* analyses of investment property yields and the Hillier Parker analyses of the same (*Average Yields*), both of which gave a UK average for late 1985 of about 10.5%, which confirms that the data does indeed represent the better end of the market.

Table 8 : V
Estimate of the industrial capital values
of the standard economic regions

Region	Floorspace ('000m²)	Average capital values (£/m²)	Total capital values (£bn)
North	23,499	100	2.350
North West	66,445	160	10.631
Yorks. and Humber.	46,042	200	9.208
East Midlands	36,732	175	6.428
West Midlands	54,317	160	8.691
East Anglia	17,439	180	3.139
South West	29,504	250	7.376
Greater London	40,636	510	20.724
South East (rest)	61,443	368	22.601
Wales	16,693	120	2.003
Scotland	30,000*	150	4.500
Great Britain	422,750	216	97.651

* Assumed

To partially offset this bias the category of building with the lowest economic value (though also the most extensive) may be taken as typical. 'Type 4 Industrial/Warehouse Units' are about 1,000m² in size and were therefore equal to the national average. They were generally about half the capital value per square metre of the most expensive units ('Small Starter Units') and about 85% of the 500m² units. Nevertheless, the total capital value in Table 8 : V, calculated on the basis of Type 4 values, must still overstate the position. The gross rental value at an average yield of 10.8% for better properties would have been about £10.5bn, or £25/m². Comparison with Table 8 : III suggests that the rent overstatement is exactly 100%, but that would be surprising. According to Hillier Parker's *Average Yields* report of November 1985 the average yield for British industrial investment (i.e., better quality) property was

10.43%, whilst the prime yield was 8%. As the average yield for all industrial property sampled in the District Valuer survey was only about 12%, this suggests that the rent difference between the better quality and the average would not have been as much as 100%. The implications of accelerating depreciation (see below) would also seem to suggest that a small over-valuation anyway would not lead to an overestimate of the site value residual.

Commercial Offices

With office property the lack of data on the spread of values does not at first sight seem such a problem. The location of offices is fairly restricted to central areas, so that the element of variability due to location is reduced. However, the variability due to the age of buildings may apply especially to offices, due to their increased rate of depreciation in the 1980s. This is highlighted in the *PMR* for Autumn 1986 (No. 46:32) in which a sharp increase over the previous year from 6.64% to 9.5% in the yields shown by office investments (excluding the City of London) is put down to this cause: 'There is some evidence to suggest that the refurbishment option is not resulting in any significantly increased capital values, and it is therefore felt that a number of purchases have been made with a view to acquiring in effect a short to medium term fixed interest security with the benefit of an opportunity to ultimately demolish and rebuild. If office obsolescence was never a serious consideration before, it must certainly now be a factor to tax the minds of investors.'

The rental values current in the previous year must therefore have failed to reflect the rents attainable upon redevelopment, and therefore fail to reflect site values. Deducing the latter from those rents must therefore lead to under-estimates.

The same point is made with regard to the industrial sector: 'As with offices, the industrial investments are looking more like short to medium term opportunities backed by site value considerations ... It seems likely [to judge from increased market activity] that sellers have resigned themselves to accepting what they can get now rather than wait any longer for some improvement in the market.'

In both these sectors then it would appear that even if the spread

Costing the Earth

of property values to the bottom end of the market were known, too strict adherence to the recorded average would under-estimate the site value residual. Particularly in the case of offices, the *PMR* indicative data for good quality accommodation erected in the previous decade would appear to provide a reasonable basis for deducing underlying land values generally.

Table 8 : VI applies this data, but for good measure reduces the rents quoted by one-fifth. The figures in *PMR 46* are used to supplement *PMR 44* (as for industry above), taking into account the year's growth which separated them. For further good measure an 8% yield is assumed rather than the 7% detected by the District

Table 8 : VI
Estimates of the aggregate commercial office rental values of the standard economic regions

Region	Office floorspace (million m²)	Average rent (£/m²)	Aggregate regional rent (£m)	Aggregate regional rent (%)
North	1.883	42.1	79.3	1.9
North West	5.824	38.6	224.7	5.3
Yorks. and Humber.	3.421	29.9	102.2	2.4
East Midlands	2.341	21.8	51.1	1.2
West Midlands	3.833	32.6	124.8	2.9
East Anglia	1.434	44.0	63.1	1.5
South West	3.527	47.3	166.8	3.9
Greater London	18.252	143.1	2612.2	61.2
City	(3.372)	(270)	(910.4)	(21.3)
Inner	(10.228)	(130)	(1329.6)	(31.1)
Outer	(4.653)	(80)	(372.2)	(8.7)
South East (rest)	8.913	67.5	601.4	14.1
Wales	1.381	34.0	46.9	1.1
Scotland	4.900*	40.0	196.0	4.6
Great Britain	55.709	76.6	4268.5	100.0

* Assumed

Valuers' sample survey. This latter yield for all offices sampled is identical to the yield in the *PMR* for offfice investments, which confirms that their rent variability must be relatively low.

Total Commercial and Industrial Land Value

The resulting capital values for Britain's commercial and industrial properties are set out in Table 8:VII. The average national yields chosen reflect the advice of surveyors and are confirmed by the findings of the DV survey. For industry it was decided to take two-thirds of the £10.5bn aggregate rent calculated from the *PMR* indicative data, and apply the average yield to that. Column (2) suggests that the DV survey was a conservative one, but it cannot be said that the *Property Market Reports* used to compile it necessarily suggest the same, because many assumptions link their data to the results.

An attempt may be made to isolate the land value portion of column (2) using CSO data. However, to apply the net capital stock figure of £153.2bn for the UK given by Bryant (1987:100) to these properties it is first necessary to form some idea of the components of land and buildings in Table 8:I, section (B). Northern Ireland, North Sea oil and gas installations, non-profit making bodies, public houses and hotels, and 'other commercial and industrial properties' are not included in Table 8:VII.

To begin with the North Sea installations, these may be taken to exhaust the private civil engineering works of the balance sheet (i.e. £17.4bn). Non profit making bodies may be deduced by making the following assumptions: that in the balance sheet's category 'commercial, industrial and other buildings', which is given for each sector, the public sector's entry (£80.5bn) contains only 'other buildings'; and that the overall asset category 'other buildings' (£100.7bn) contains only non-profit making bodies other than public sector buildings. The difference (£20.2bn) must therefore be the figure we are looking for. This leaves £31.6bn in the personal sector's 'commercial, industrial and other buildings' category, which in fact leaves the right amount of commercial and industrial buildings for the rest of the private sector.

Only Scotland and Northern Ireland remain to be subtracted to

Table 8 : VII
Comparison with the District Valuers' estimate of the capital value of Great Britain's industrial and commercial property (end-1985)

Sector	(1) District Valuers' sample survey with Scottish data from column (2) added (£bn)	(2) British capital values (£bn)	(3) Assumed average yield in column (2) (%)
Shops and restaurants	61.5	86.6	8
Commercial offices	51.5	69.6	8
Industry and warehouses	48.5	57.8	12
Great Britain	161.5	214.0	

leave the grand total produced by the District Valuers' sample survey. Their land and buildings must therefore be the residual, which is £27.2bn. At 13.6% of the UK equivalent this seems rather high, as they contributed only 10.9% to the Gross Domestic Product. The Northern Ireland proportion will be taken as £5bn.

Finally, public houses and hotels in the UK, and 'other commercial and industrial buildings,' may be estimated by extending the DV survey of England and Wales results in proportion to population, that is to £16.7bn and £12.5bn, respectively.

The net capital stocks contained in these totals will be assumed to be equal to the DV survey's overall 69% share, except that the North Sea installations are all net capital. This means subtracting £54.9bn from the UK figure, which leaves £98.3bn as the net capital of the properties in Tables 8 : IV to 8 : VII.

Subtracting this figure from the total in column (2) of Table 8 : VII leaves £115.7bn as the capital value of British industrial and commercial land at the end of 1985.

The Question of Depreciation

It should be recalled that the CSO net capital stock figure may be an over-estimate, and that in the DV survey the buildings may have been over-valued. These possibilities may be broadly checked by reference to the Royal Institution of Chartered Surveyors' Building Cost Information Service. In the *BCIS Quarterly Review of Building Prices* (February 1986) average UK building costs per square metre are given for various types of buildings in the 4th Quarter of 1985. These do not include site works, garages or professional fees, but such information is provided by the DoE for council houses (DoE/SDD/WO 1986 : 82,84,88), where they appear to account for over one-third of the price. Neither do they apply to central London, where building costs are twice as high as the general level. The figures in Table 8 : VIII have therefore been calculated using 160% of the BCIS averages and doubling the cost of 6m m² of office space.

Table 8 : VIII
Comparison of the gross replacement cost of industrial and commercial floorspace in England and Wales with the implied net replacement cost of the District Valuers' survey

Asset	UK average replacement cost ($£/m^2$)	Total replacement cost ($£bn$)	DV survey building value (net replacement cost, $£bn$)
Shops and restaurants	480	39	37
Commercial offices	768	44	34
Factories and warehouses (excl. open storage)	384	142	30
Total	n.a.	225	101

The figures are so rough that the only judgement that can be made from them is that the DV assessments of the net value of commercial buildings look too high if the gross replacement cost estimates are anywhere near the truth. As a check, applying the average cost of tenders for housing accepted by local authorities in England and Wales ($440/m²) to 1540m m² of UK housing floorspace gives a gross replacement cost of $677.6bn. This compares with $526bn in the Blue Book's Table 11.9. From this it would seem that the gross estimates are unlikely to be an underestimate.

Vacant Land

Land which was not included in these calculations but which nevertheless has a value is vacant land. The floorspace statistics do not include properties which have been demolished (or 'deroofed', as the case may be in districts where a rate is levied on vacant properties).

The 'deindustrialisation' of the previous decade undoubtedly contributed a significant proportion of industrial land to Britain's 'wasting acres'. Between 1974 and 1985 manufacturing employment in the UK declined by 30%, manufacturing output by 10%, and industrial floorspace in England and Wales by 5%. Meanwhile, the whole economy grew by 17% (GDP at constant factor cost), and warehousing and commercial floorspace by 29%.

Between 1974 and 1985 the official figure for 'derelict land' in England (i.e. despoiled and in need of treatment before beneficial use) increased by about 6%, to reach a total of 45,683 ha, 46% of which was urban. For the seven major conurbations the tally increased by 28% to 14,746 ha, due notably to the run-down of industry (Chisholm and Kivell 1987:16-19).

This data does not include land that is unused, vacant or waste, even though it is not severely damaged. In 1977 the Civic Trust estimated that there were an additional 100,000 ha of 'dormant' urban land in Britain which could be made useable with very little reclamation cost (Cantell 1977). Ten years later, Chisholm and Kivell reckoned that 'There is some measure of agreement among independent analysts that a figure of 210,000 ha represents a fair estimate of the combined total of derelict and vacant land in public and private ownership.' This estimate was for England and it was implied (1987 : 24) that perhaps three-quarters or more constituted urban land. Bruton and Gore identified a further 4,000ha of vacant urban land in South Wales in 1979, and the pro rata figure for Scotland would have been about 8,000 ha.

In his survey of the area of publicly-owned land in Britain in early 1973 Dowrick (1974) included under municipal ownership a category of 'miscellaneous holdings' which covered the following: 'suburbs or rural areas, title to which has long been vested in the local authority or freeman, and overlapping them ... such items as land acquired for planning and redevelopment, or for conservation, or reclamation, for markets, depots, lavatories, baths, car parks, even gypsy sites, as well as for magistrates courts and probation offices. Pro rata estimates for these residual holdings: at least 65,000ha, at most 121,400ha'. These land banks would in the main be classified as vacant land. Local authorities probably own at least one-third of all such land, so the figures cited are consistent with those above.

If we postulate 165,000ha of derelict and vacant urban land in Britain in 1985, that would have constituted 10% of the urban area (excluding transport land outside settlements). Burrows' estimate for metropolitan areas in the mid-1970s was 5%, and Bruton and Gore's for urban South Wales in 1979 'just over 5%'.

Not all of this land is developable. A survey conducted by the GLC in 1984 indicated a total of 3,000ha of 'developable land in London which was vacant, under-used or derelict.' Of this only 26% was judged as suitable for housing. An aerial survey in 1982, also for the GLC, identified 1,800 parcels of land over 0.25ha in size totalling 4,791ha which appeared to be 'vacant, under-used or derelict.' Of this area only 30% was judged 'developable' (Inner City Commission 1987:11). Of the 40,235ha of publicly-owned vacant lots over 0.4ha in size on the Land Registers in 1987, 42.3% was classified as having 'high development potential' (Hall 1987: 14).

This assortment of evidence justifies us in taking 50,000ha as a round figure for vacant urban land with development potential in Britain in 1985. How this area is divided between potential commercial, industrial and residential uses is not of great consequence for the final outcome of this study. Industrial and residential sites are of similar average values and they would account for nearly all of it. However, the division of the area by original use does matter for the purpose of this chapter, which is to test the estimates in the previous chapter. In that chapter the areas were taken from calculations which had been compiled without separating vacant land, and so they include land which has gone out of use and not yet been allocated to other uses. It is necessary, therefore, to add a valuation of vacant industrial and commercial sites to the results in this chapter. Assuming an equal split between industrial and residential uses prior to land becoming vacant, and the same commercial proportion as with land currently in use (i.e. 2.8% of urban land, excluding rural routeways), then the valuation is as in Table 8:IX, which comes to £10.1bn.

Table 8 : IX
Valuation of developable vacant land in Britain in 1985 by previous use

Previous use	Area (ha)	Value (£' 000/ha)	Total value (£bn)
Commerce	1,400	2,360	3.3
Industry	24,300	278	6.8
Housing	24,300	277	6.7
	50,000	n.a.	16.8

'Other' Commercial and Industrial Land

Public houses, hotels and boarding houses, commercial and lock-up garages, holiday camps, some mineral hereditaments, and sundry commercial properties are also not included in the DoE's floor-space statistics, though they are included in the area data used in Chapter 7. An estimate for these must therefore be made in this chapter. Though we have argued above that site values were considerably under-estimated by the District Valuers' survey we can do no better than rely on its findings in this instance. Pro rata extension of the total value for these properties in that survey produces a figure of about £29bn for Britain. Applying the survey's general site value proportion of 31% gives a total land value of £9bn.

The Final Total For Britain

The estimated value of the commercial and industrial land relating to the DoE's floorspace statistics was £115.7bn. Adding the estimated values for vacant land (£10.1bn) and 'other' commercial and industrial properties (£9bn) produces a figure of £134.8bn. The method of calculation used in the previous chapter for the equivalent land produced a figure of £143.2bn.

It is only to be expected that the residual method of calculation should have produced a lower total than the spatial method of calculation. It measures existing use site values as opposed to full development site values. However, the application of the method in this chapter has been a compromise, for rental levels on fully developed sites, often in prime locations, have provided the foundation stones of our valuations. To what extent the assumed gradients of values from these sites have accurately reflected both existing under-use of sites and their inferior locations we cannot tell. Nevertheless it is a source of comfort that the final result should lie between this study's full development estimate and official estimates of existing use values.

9

Mineral Resources and Land Used for Public Services

DAVID RICHARDS

In its Attempt to calculate the wealth of the nation the Central Statistical Office has been hampered by a 'paucity of information' for some sectors, 'in particular for local authorities for which valuations are perhaps weakest' (Bryant 1987: 101). The position is affirmed by the Audit Commission, which states that 'the full extent of local authority property holdings in England and Wales is unknown' (1988: 1).

The Audit Commission has, however, suggested that the value of local authority land and buildings, excluding houses, amounts to more than £100 billion. This figure was calculated thus (in 1987): the annual debt charge related to property is over £2.5bn, which implies a residual debt value, or a historic cost less depreciation property value, of some £25bn; multiplying by four converts approximately to current prices. But the result is regarded as an underestimate. John Banham, the Controller of the Audit, stated in 1986 that these assets are 'probably worth of the order of £200 billion' (1986: letter).

Central government is somewhat better informed about its assets. The annual reports of the Property Services Agency (PSA) contain floorspace statistics for the UK Civil Estate, and what Bryant (1987: 116) called 'a desk valuation' was made in 1982. This came up with an estimate of 'about £3bn' (personal communication). The office floorspace was 7.2m m² in March 1985, which was 11.4% of all office floorspace, excluding Scotland and Northern Ireland's commercial and local government offices (PSA 1987: 35). Total floorspace was 11.6m m², equivalent to 2.2% of industrial and commercial floorspace in England and Wales. Area figures are not available, however, except for the Defence Estate, which may be assumed to be already included in other land uses.

Floorspace statistics are available from the Department of the Environment and the Welsh Office for local government offices in England and Wales. In 1985 they amounted to 5.3m m², which extended pro rata would be almost 6m m² for the UK — slightly less than the central government equivalent.

To estimate the areas of the various public land uses the information gleaned for public sector holdings in 1972/3 by Professor F. E. Dowrick (1974) has been combined with the relevant details from Table 4 : VII. The following assumptions have been made to complete the coverage: that one-fifth must be added to Dowrick's schools and one-tenth to hospitals to allow for private provision (CSO 1987:57, 132; Inland Revenue 1986:79); half of the land used by education and the police is playing fields and therefore 'open space'; central government occupies as much as the 2,200-odd ha estimated by Dowrick for all local government offices, libraries and museums (in view of the floorspace statistics); church premises occupy 4,000 ha; and the value of residential estate roads is included in the value of houses (Bryant 1987:117).

With these adjustments Dowrick's figure for public buildings and institutions in 1972/3 becomes 79,000 ha, as against 77,000 ha for 1985 in Table 4 : VII.

Placing a value on these areas requires an even broader brush treatment. However, the average capital value of housing land in Britain in 1985, ascertained in Chapter 6, provides a bedrock upon which a tentative structure of values may be erected. Table 9 : I sets up such a structure by suggesting the opportunity cost of current land uses. Public utilities are not included as they were valued on a par with industry in Chapter 7.

As a check on the results, the local authority share (including all open space and roads) amounts to £42.1bn, which is 21.1% of John Banham's high estimate for the value of buildings and land. This seems reasonable.

Also, according to a National Audit Office report (NAO 1988:6), the hospital estate in England comprises 2,000 buildings and more than 50,000 acres (20,243 ha). In 1985-86 the capital value

Table 9 : I
The value of land used for public services

Land use	Area ('000 ha)	At (£'000/ha)	Total value (£m)
Education land (minus playing fields), hospitals and prisons	62	277 (housing values)	17,174
Government offices, social services, libraries, museums, police and fire stations, churches	15	1,180 (about half of commercial values[1])	17,700
Urban transport land (other than residential estate roads)	114	111 (two-fifths of housing values[2])	12,654
Rural transport land	343	2.61 (agricultural values[2])	895
Urban open space	230	69.25 (say 25% of housing[2])	15,928
Total	764		64,351

1. See Chapter 7, Table 7:V.
2. Reflecting Inland Revenue Valuation Office advice (Bryant 1987:117).

of the buildings was estimated at £13bn, with the sites worth well in excess of £4.5bn. This broadly confirms the hospital valuation in Table 9:I, though it suggests that it may be on the high side.

Mineral Resources

The Central Statistical Office has been unable to assess subsoil deposits 'largely because of the difficulties of valuation' (Bryant 1987:108). However, the effects of volatile prices and fluctuating estimates of reserves on capital values need not worry us here as it is the annual economic rent that ultimately concerns us.

As the general public is once again largely in the position of 'owner', one would expect the government to be rack renting the commercial mining companies and that the annual value of the nation's minerals would be evident. This is not the case, however. Again the British people are unaware of the annual worth of the assets that belong to them.

Peter Lilley, Economic Secretary to the Treasury (1987-), has proposed reforms. He has written,

> auctioning the licenses subject to a known tax regime for future discoveries ... is the only way to extract, on behalf of the public, 100% of the value of the North Sea oil rights attributable to them as owners whilst leaving sufficient incentive for efficient exploration and development.

This is done in America — where private landowners showed the way — but

> in Britain we have almost always given away licences subject to a fixed royalty and a uniform oil tax regime (albeit a more severe one than operates in the U.S.A. or Canada).

On the U.S. outer continental shelf in the quarter century up to 1978

> the cumulative receipts from lease sales, royalties and rentals, but not including corporation tax on profits, amounted to 70% of the total value of all oil and gas so far produced' (Lilley 1980: 24, 25, 5, 17).

Government revenue from the North Sea (including corporation tax), having risen more slowly than output, and destined to decline more rapidly, peaked in 1985 at only about 60% of the annual value of output (*Financial Times*, 12 February 1985). Garnaut and Clunies Ross agree with Lilley's view that 'it seems a mistake to forgo the extra revenue that might be raised by auctioning licences' — and, they add, by 'a simpler additional tax more closely related to profitability' (1983: 293).

Three token auctions of exploration licences have taken place. In the ninth licensing round, in 1984/5, 15 blocks were sold for £120m while the remaining 180 blocks were offered for discretionary allocation. Only 78 of the latter were licensed, but if these had raised on average half as much as the blocks sold they would have realized another £300m for the British public.

Figures from the Brown Book of 1986 suggest that up to two-thirds of the value of British oil and gas production in 1985 may well

Figure 9 : I
Derivation of British Coal's land rent

PRODUCTION COSTS - £s PER TONNE

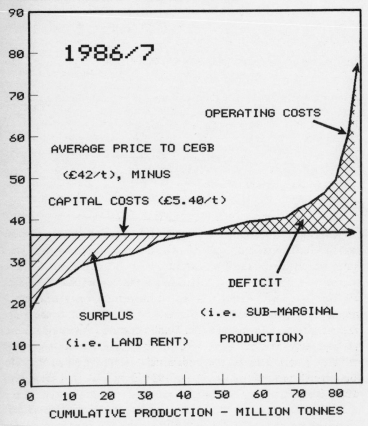

CUMULATIVE PRODUCTION - MILLION TONNES

Source: Financial Times (1987 : 2, 4).

have been 'land value', or economic rent (i.e., sales minus all production costs): 'The overall average cost per barrel is £7 ($9) for all the fields currently in production on the UKCS ... These estimates are based on production and costs before payment of royalties and taxes. They include the costs of exploration, development and operation over the expected life of the fields, but exclude abortive exploration costs not attributable to individual fields. A real return on capital of 10% is assumed' (Dept. of Energy 1986 : 58-9).

As the average price per barrel of oil in 1985 was £21 — the volume of output being 0.962bn barrels (Dept of Energy 1986 : 2) and its value £20.291bn (British Geological Survey 1987 : 1) — the surplus over production costs was £14 per barrel, or £13.47bn in total.

Comparable figures are not published for natural gas production, but if the same proportions apply this would add another £1.2bn to annual economic rent in 1985. The Gas Levy, designed to recoup from British Gas some of the economic rent that it captures as the mining companies' sole outlet, raised about £0.5bn in 1985 (British Gas Corporation 1986 : 21).

Coal and other minerals also have to be considered. In Scotland 'operators have paid as much as 450% of agricultural value' for coal bearing land, 'in addition to the royalty paid to the National Coal Board' (IRVO Autumn 1985 : 78). The NCB records the net book value of its mines and land at around £1bn (NCB 1986 : 40), and Figure 9 : I indicates that their annual land value may be about £0.3bn. The shape of the graph, however, suggests that small improvements in operating efficiency would give more than pro rata increases in economic rent. £0.5bn should easily be possible, perhaps even £1bn a year. Here we shall take the middle figure because it corresponds to a traditional $12\frac{1}{2}$% royalty on production, which was worth £3.899bn in 1985 (British Geological Survey 1987 : 1).

A $12\frac{1}{2}$% royalty on the value of the rest of UK mineral production in 1985 would have yielded £0.183bn. The total mineral land rental value for the UK in 1985 by these calculations, therefore, was £15.353bn. Pro rata for GB this becomes £14.93bn.

10
Conclusions and Recommendations

THE FIVE years up to 1990 were characterised by frenzied activity in the urban land market, a period reminiscent of the speculative boom of the early 1970s. That was one reason why, for the purpose of this study, we chose 1985: it was the most recent year when the land market was 'normal', in terms of the secular trends. The housing market illustrates this point. We placed a value of £139.7bn on residential land in the South-East, which constituted 58% of the total. The value of that land rose markedly from 1986. By 1988, acres in the South-East worth £2,000 as farmland were fetching £1m or more with planning permission to build houses. Our calculations based on 1985 values provide a sound baseline from which to extrapolate trends, which reveal that rent has increased dramatically as a proportion of national income (Table 2:II).

The methodology employed has been one of simple arithmetic, aggregating the quantity of land in particular uses, and multiplying these by values which we derived from both Inland Revenue and market sources. Where assumptions had to be made, these were biased in favour of caution. One result is that the capital value of land — which we place at £505bn (excluding minerals) — is understated. For example, we valued residential land on the basis of the number of housing units. This approach fails to take full account of the 'hope' value of land that is coloured 'pink' on the planner's map, land which the owners hold in the expectation of one day converting cornfields into construction sites. That value is, of course, traded, and therefore 'bankable' but it is not measured in our assessment of the agricultural sector.

Further Research

We provide the first authoritative guide to the value of Britain's natural resources, which enables us to challenge the reliability of some of the official figures. This is notable in the case of industrial and commercial land, which the Central Statistical Office estimated to be £85bn. Our figure is £143bn, which specialists in this type of property intuitively felt was an *under-estimate*.

Further research to resolve such controversies is essential. The government accepted a recommendation by the House of Commons Treasury and Civil Service Committee (1988:x) that the reliability of statistics in the national accounts should be investigated. MPs, alarmed at the range of residual errors in the official data, described the situation as 'disturbing'. The implications are critical:

> Without a clear statistical account of how the economy behaved last year it stands to reason that Treasury officials are ill-placed to forecast how the economy will perform this year.

The value of such a review of the statistics, however, turns on whether the appropriate variables are being measured. Policies cannot be rationally formulated without a sound quantitative assessment of the *relevant* influences on the market. The land market constitutes an area of unparalleled ignorance. Yet its impact on the markets which regulate labour and capital is of crucial significance. Land displays certain characteristics that are unique. For example, the trend in the price of land over the medium term is upwards. Property (because it incorporates a large land value component) outperforms other assets in the long run. The share of national income going to rent increases, while the share to 'profits' — meaning the returns to capital, properly defined as man-made artefacts — decreases, over the course of 20-year business cycles (Harrison 1983). The present findings verify this hypothesis.

The motives for investing in land, and the consequences for the rest of the economy, are distinctive but generally disguised by the absence of information. For example, the DoE (1988:27) takes the view that 'Speculative hoarding is not seen as a major problem'.

No evidence was adduced in support of that perception. This is not surprising.

> The problem overall is that much of our knowledge is based on case studies of limited geographical extent and that our understanding of the wider incidence and relative importance of all these factors is very limited (DoE 1988 : 29).

Nonetheless, the notion that land speculation is not a major problem can be challenged by studies that pinpoint this phenomenon as having a significant bearing on the economy. Consider, for instance, the investigation by the National Audit Office (1988 : 3) into the National Health Service's use of property. It found that the NHS had hoarded land 'for long periods on the advice of the District Valuer in the hope that sale values might improve'; one in five health districts confirmed that at least 40% of their land was disposable. This speculation in real estate may be rational from the point of view of the individual property owner, but may not be the best policy when judged against considerations of social welfare. But how does the underuse of precious natural resources affect the nation? An impressionistic answer was offered by the Audit Commission (1988 : 17), which expressed this view after examining the propensity of local authorities to hold land in a vacant state:

> Land is frequently held 'in advance of need' when the authority has no coherent plan for its exploitation and there is little likelihood of making the necessary resources available for development. As a result, the authority locks up land with development potential which could be exploited by others with benefits for the community as a whole.

It would seem to be incumbent on District Valuers and councillors to justify a strategy of 'idling' land that would otherwise be used for the construction of homes, offices or factories. But given the present state of the art, how can we adjudicate on the conflict between the individual's interests and the wider claims of society, unless the fullest information is available as to the quantities and values involved? We can only guess at the social costs and benefits of what has been a lackadaisical approach to managing the nation's resources.

It is evident that a new primacy should be accorded to data on the land market. Otherwise, there is the risk of an escalation in the reported practice of writing confidentiality clauses into contracts, which 'prevent publicity of property deals' (*Estates Times*, February 26, 1988). The free flow of information is a pre-condition of an efficient market. The ownership and value of shares traded on the stock exchange are openly recorded in the public files; and there is no attempt to disguise the identities of employees who dispose of their labour, or the value of their wages and salaries. We cannot discern any special reasons why the land market should be shrouded in the secrecy which inevitably limits its efficiency.

A New Domesday Book

Ultimately, there can be no substitute for on-site inspection of land values. Britain needs a new Domesday Book. A nationwide assessment of natural resources may sound a daunting task, but it would be a brave man who suggested that what was possible in the time of the Normans would not be possible in the age of the micro-chip!

The Inland Revenue established a Valuation Office as long ago as the First World War, after Parliament had ordered that natural resources should be valued for fiscal purposes. Although the relevant legislation was allowed to lapse it was nonetheless decided to retain the Office, which exists to this day. Recently, one of its valuers was asked about the feasibility of valuing land on a nationwide basis. He replied:

> Provided the ground rules were clearly established I do not think that the valuation process itself would present any greater problems than those of the present (rating) system (Fenwick 1987).

In fact, according to a study by the Land Institute (1974), the process would be simpler and cheaper to undertake than that of valuing both land and buildings as required by the rating system. We believe the costs to be within the realms of practical politics; they would not exceed the charge imposed by the need to compile the register for the Poll Tax (estimated by the AMA/ADC [1988] at £144m). The money spent on acquiring a complete valuation of one of the three factors employed in the productive process would rapidly repay itself by greater efficiency.

It was with this in mind that Henry S. Reuss, who at the time was chairman of the House Committee on Banking, Finance and Urban Affairs, proposed in 1978 that the U.S. Government should establish a comprehensive land price index. His arguments are worth restating for the light they cast on our recommendation that more information on the land market should be provided through official sources.

Reuss contended that land prices were rising 'more rapidly than almost any other element in the economy,' and yet were largely ignored in dealing with inflation generally or the escalating prices of housing, food and other products in which land was a significant factor. For example, in the 30 years after 1949, the Consumer Price Index rose by 300%; the price of the typical new single-family house went up by 500%; but the price of the land under that house increased by 1,275%. A land price index was a 'useful first step' in alerting officials and the public to the role of land in the economy, making it more likely that appropriate changes in taxes and other policies would be proposed and eventually enacted. Despite a great deal of scholarly research stemming from this political initiative, the federal government in Washington does not yet have at its command the vital tool of a national land price index (see Chapter 12).

Until the British government assumes its responsibility for carrying out the task of providing such information, scholars in academia and researchers in the private sector will have to do the best they can with the material at hand. In this connection, the land price index published in the DoE's *Housing and Construction Statistics* series lags well behind market developments, and the research in the Inland Revenue's *Property Market Report* is updated only twice a year. As a result, official land market data is of interest to the historian but of little use to analysts and policy-makers who are supposed to keep abreast of rapidly changing market conditions.

A Cadastral Survey

The imprecision of the statistics on land use is a national scandal. We have compiled an assessment of the amount of land in the various categories of usage which we believe to be the best available.

Nonetheless, a full cadastral survey is urgently required. Married with the information being collated annually by the staff of the Ordnance Survey for the Department of the Environment, on the rate of change of land usage, accurate information on the stock would confirm, in our view, the buoyancy of land as a source of income.

But there is another urgent reason why the government should finance a cadastral survey. Major political decisions affecting land use will have to be taken within the next few years. Inactivity will itself constitute a decision with far-reaching consequences, so there is no way of dodging the problem. Perhaps the most dramatic example is the prospect of change in agriculture. If member governments of the European Economic Community pursue their radical proposals for reducing the subsidies and protection accorded to farmers, an estimated one million acres would no longer be used to produce food in Britain. But even if the governments fail to agree on substantive reforms to the Common Agricultural Policy, the rate of increase in productivity ($2\frac{1}{2}\%$ *per annum*) will dictate the need to 'idle' a great deal of farmland just to restrict food surpluses to their present levels (Agriculture EDC : 1987). Decisions with such sweeping effects on the rural environment ought to be taken with the benefit of the most precise information.

We are conscious of the fact that, in recent years, the amount of money spent by government on research has been husbanded. We would point out, however, that a cadastral survey cannot be regarded as an optional extra to the process of policy-making. Without the information, decisions could be taken with fearful results, which would be felt over an inter-generational timescale. The Thatcher government has not limited the expenditure of public funds where it has deemed such spending to be necessary to implement departures from previous practice. For example, it has been willing to accept the increased costs of administering the Poll Tax, which are calculated by the AMA/ADC to be two-and-a-half times more expensive than the previous approach to raising revenue for local government through the tax on property.[1]

Towards New Policies

The quality of decisions taken by Parliament on contemporary issues of major significance would have been enhanced by the availability of more data on the land market. To illustrate the thesis that the impact of the land market penetrates deeper into policy-making than is generally appreciated, we focus on four of these issues.

(i) Free markets

The Conservative Government which came to power in 1979 placed the primacy of the market mechanism at the centre of its economic programme. It judged the strategy of previous governments, which favoured a greater degree of State involvement in the economy, to have failed. Nine years later the Chancellor of the Exchequer was moved to claim that 'the transformation of Britain's economic performance during the 1980s, a transformation now acknowledged throughout the world, is above all due to the supply-side reforms we have introduced to allow markets of all kinds to work better' (Lawson 1988).

This pronouncement came at the end of nine months during which the housing market presented the economy with serious problems. The cost of housing, forced up, in the main, by the restricted supply of land, distorted the labour market. Wages were higher than they need have been and employees were prevented from moving about the country in response to the availability of jobs; the credit boom — fuelled by accelerating prices in the housing market — destabilised the balance of Britain's foreign trade; and the capital markets were thrown into a state of uncertainty, as the Chancellor sought to deal with the problem by raising interest rates (Bover *et al*. 1988). All of this was due primarily to the power exercised by those who operate the residential land market! Evidently, there was considerable scope for reforms to encourage efficiency in the distribution of resources within the property sub-markets.

Critics of government policy maintained that the problems were further aggravated by the decision to abolish rates on residential properties: relief from the property tax was predicted to raise house prices by an average of 20%, and by considerably more in London.

That the property market was not functioning efficiently, whatever the success achieved by the government in other markets, was clear from the depth of dissatisfaction within the ranks of the Conservative Party itself. Many backbench MPs vociferously objected to the decision by the Environment Secretary (Nicholas Ridley) to allow more construction on greenfield sites.

Most observers agreed that, if it were possible, new construction ought to take place on re-cycled land in the cities. The debate, however, was bedevilled by an absence of precise information on whether sufficient land *was* available. Builders complained that they had insufficient land at their disposal; the government said sufficient land was zoned to meet development needs.

Related to this area of controversy was the problem of whether the pricing mechanism was doing its job. Evidently it was not, for the Environment Secretary (Lean 1988) suggested that he was disposed to use *force majeure* to unlock land that was being withheld from those who wanted to build houses in the cities. The point to which we wish to draw attention is this. The most accurate indication of the wishes of prospective house buyers is the price of land, which — if the market were operating freely — responds to demand. One precondition for an effective operation of the pricing mechanism is the full and free flow of relevant information. The fact that land was no longer affordable for many families who needed homes suggests a serious defect somewhere in the allocative mechanism.

(ii) The Poll Tax

A revealing argument was employed by the Prime Minister, Margaret Thatcher, during the Parliamentary debate on the Poll Tax as a substitute for the rating system. Objections to the government's proposal to change the revenue-raising system for local authorities were met with the counter-claim that no alternative to the Poll Tax had been adequately advocated. If there is substance to this defence of the Poll Tax, it arises solely from the fact that information was not available to explain how the rating system could be reformed to everyone's satisfaction.

There have been a variety of criticisms of the integrity of the rating system.[2] The overriding objection is that, insofar as the tax falls on the value of a building, it is a disincentive to investment in improvements in living and working conditions. This suggests the need to untax that portion of a property's value that is due to improvements on the land.[3] The tax revenue could then be derived from site values alone, which is the form of rating system employed by a large number of municipalities in Australia. The dynamic benefits of such a reform are alluded to by the DoE (1988 : 39), which discussed the problem of dealing with vacant land in Britain's inner cities. It noted that 'because land without buildings is unrated, they (rates) do nothing to stimulate the re-use of vacant land'.

Such a proposal for reform of the rating system has in the past been met with the fair objection that information was not available on whether land constituted a sufficiently buoyant source of income to finance the needs of local authorities. We now know that the rental income of land exclusive of capital improvements is more than sufficient to underwrite the costs of locally-administered services. An alternative to the Poll Tax can now be seen as a realistic possibility, if the political demand for it existed.

But previous attempts to reform the rating system in favour of a site-value only tax have been met with the objection that such a property tax is unworkable. In this connection, it is worth noting some international practices.

Land is valued apart from the capital improvements upon it in countries as economically and culturally diverse as Australia and Taiwan, and as geographically dispersed as New Zealand and Jamaica. Perhaps the model worthy of immediate study, because of the convenient access to information, is Denmark (see Appendix 3). There, the system of land valuation has been part of the government's responsibilities for over seven decades. The data on a site-by-site basis are so accessible to the public, that they are now even published in the Danish equivalent of the Yellow Pages (Harrison 1988 : 19). This accessibility to information on land values, and the meticulous system of public records, facilitates the housing market and cuts the transaction costs to consumers.

The introduction of computers for the 1981 revaluation enabled valuers in Denmark to improve their efficiency. They generate assessments that are extremely close to market prices. Table 10:I indicates the correspondence between the assessed value and sales price, which by 1986 were for all practical purposes identical for residential properties.

Table 10 : I
Denmark: difference between assessed value and sales prices: %

	Single-family homes	Summer houses
1973	–10	–40
1977	–7	–21
1981	–5	0
1986	–3	–1

We find, then, confirmation of a fact that is acknowledged among Britain's professional valuers: the assessment of land is a skill which yields results of the highest possible accuracy.[4]

(iii) Impact of tax cuts

The Thatcher government placed a high priority on cutting tax rates, with the aim of stimulating the supply-side of the economy. While it is not clear that the taxpayers were the principal beneficiaries, there is now abundant evidence that the strategy served to subvert the supply-side reforms in the labour and capital markets. The starting point of any analysis has to be Ricardian rent theory which, as we saw in Chapter 1, predicts that an increase in net income is to some degree offset by a rise in rents payable to landowners, leaving the real disposable income at or near the former level. This suggests that, to be effective, a tax-cutting fiscal strategy requires a mechanism for neutralising the capacity of the *land-owning rentier* to appropriate the gains.

A study by the Department of the Environment concluded that the main taxes affecting urban land markets were Corporation Tax, the Rates and Value Added Tax. What happens if, say, the Corporation Tax rate is lowered?

> The lower the level of Corporation Tax, the greater a company's bargaining power in terms of financial resources available to bid up rents in order to secure and retain the premises of its choice. Landlords benefit twice over ... (DoE 1988 : 39)

Whether the added bargaining power rests with the beneficiary of a tax cut, or the landowner who is in a position to exact a greater share of someone else's fiscal good fortune, need not detain us here. The outcome remains the same: the price of land rises to absorb the gains from the Chancellor of the Exchequer's decision to cut taxes. Thus, while the government thought it had 'no policy measures directed towards land prices' (DoE 1988 : 54), an inescapable consequence of the Thatcher administration's tax-cutting policy was that land prices were driven up.

This power places an awesome responsibility on government. In recent years, the direct impact of a number of important government policies on the price of land has been ignored; the potential consequences did not feature in any of the parliamentary debates that preceded the enactment of the laws. Yet these policies constituted a systematic redistribution of income in favour of land owners. Major fiscal implications flow from this ability to increase the economic rent of land — a power, we stress, that is regularly exercised, though usually from a starting point of ignorance. Two of these are identified here.

(i) A government that wished to cut taxes that fall on labour and capital, as part of its economic strategy (for example, in the pursuit of full employment: lower taxes ought to expand the demand for goods and services, in turn stimulating new investment and employment) could only succeed if it prevented the fiscal benefits from leaking into higher property prices. This leakage has been identified as a serious obstacle to supply-side programmes: see, for example, Gilder (1981). A tax on the rent of land is the only mechanism that would neutralise the propensity of the land owner to appropriate the taxpayers' windfall gains without further disrupting economic activity. The success of this policy would depend on the rate at which the tax was levied. To deter landowners from snatching the increase in people's disposable incomes, the tax rate would have to be high, with a compensating reduction in the rate of other taxes.

(ii) Economists as far back as Adam Smith argue that a tax on land values is superior to other taxes, in that it does not represent an obstacle to the wealth-creating process (through, for example, the impact on the price of products, and the motivation of people to work). A government that wished to enhance living standards by improving the performance of the economy could do so by substituting the tax on land values for other taxes. This rationalisation of the tax structure could be accomplished with the minimum of disruption. During the transitional phase, the buoyancy of rent as a tax base could be regulated by the rate at which the burden of other taxes was reduced.

(iv) Consumer Choice

Higher prices restrict consumer choice. This is not necessarily so in the labour and capital markets, where higher prices signal a shortage and so attract a fresh supply. This response tends to moderate prices. Where the supply of a particular factor is scarce, rising prices operate as a rationing mechanism, thereby ensuring an efficient allocation of resources.

The land market, however, where the factor in question is relatively fixed in supply, is unique: rising prices encourage owners to withhold their sites, speculating on the prospect of an even higher capital gain in the future. The eyesore sites — hundreds of them in prime locations in most cities of the western world — bear witness to this phenomenon.

The amount of vacant land in Britain increased during the 1970s and early 1980s. There was no shortage of valuable sites in central locations available for development by the private sector. Prices, therefore, ought to have *decreased* to levels that would have made these sites attractive to investors. That the market and the pricing mechanism were not working satisfactorily is evident from the fact that the government deemed it necessary to establish new bureaucracies (urban development corporations) equipped with draconian powers and charged with the task of prizing some of these sites out of the hands of owners and placing them at the disposal of prospective users. Ironically, however, far from injecting fresh competition into the land market, the government unwittingly formulated policies that helped to raise the price of land to unaffordable levels. A case in point is the Enterprise Zones, where firms received government grants and tax allowances for capital expenditure and relief from local rates.

> The capital allowance concession increases the rate of return to developers and again tends to feed through into higher land values. The rates concession represents a direct saving to tenants (and owner occupiers) but there is evidence that it is largely offset by higher rental values, which in turn feed through into capital and land values. (DoE 1988 : 40).

Consumer choice was similarly restricted by government policy. The decision to abolish rates on residential properties, starting with Scotland in 1989, is illustrative. The scale of the rise in the price of land was controversial. The government predicted that house prices (which effectively meant residential land prices) would rise by about 5% (DoE 1986 : 102). Economists in universities and the City suggested a more marked rise, reaching 20% or more in the London area. One of these noted that 'The wider economic effects are uncertain but likely to be very significant' (Spencer 1988 : 1), citing threats to the supply-side of the economy as a major consequence of the decision to abolish the residential property tax. So far as we know from the public debates on the replacement tax, the 'community charge' or Poll Tax, this impact was a wholly incidental effect of the government's change in the system of raising revenue for local authorities. Yet coming at a time when housing land prices in the South-East already exceeded £1m an acre, the government-induced rises had a significant effect in raising house prices to unaffordable levels, and so retarding the extension of home ownership.

Governments may consider it right that there should be losers and gainers as a result of the promulgation of new laws. At present, because of the imperfections in, and a shortage of information about, the land market, people's incomes, economic prospects and asset values are altered by a process that is largely covert. In a democracy, the electorate is entitled to have the full accounts of government decisions at its disposal, so that the politicians can be challenged. Governments which seek to influence the economy should be similarly concerned to know how they are affecting the value and distribution of the real estate of the nation.

NOTES

1   The possibility of an economical compilation of property market data is illustrated by British Telecom's Video Map Imaging System, a computerised map-based property search system. Ordnance Survey maps are stored on video discs, and can be accessed in seconds by using a keyboard and colour monitor. The system was developed for Land Registry offices, providing rapid and cheap access to records. By linking estate agents and solicitors into the system, a nationwide database of current prices and useage could be established at a very low cost and no delay. For the first time in history, the property market could systematically derive comprehensive indices of values of the sort that are taken for granted by dealers on the Stock Exchange! Chorley (1987) provides a comprehensive account of the methods and technology at our disposal for collating geographic information.

2   We exclude the criticism about large increases in the rates liability for some property owners, following revaluation (which first made itself felt in Scotland in 1987). This discontent is wholly the responsibility of successive governments which chose to postpone revaluations; the dissatisfaction does not arise from an intrinsic defect in the property tax *per se*. If revaluations had taken place on a regular basis, in accordance with sound fiscal practice, the changes in tax liability — both upwards and downwards, in line with movements in property prices — would have taken the form of small, manageable increments.

3   Alternatively, the depressive effect on construction generated by an undifferentiated property tax could be mitigated by a progressive transfer of the burden away from the value of capital improvements and on to land values. This is the course adopted by some cities in Pennsylvania, including Pittsburgh — the city which Prince Charles, among others, has commended for its rehabilitation of the built environment.

Table 10 : II

Two-rate tax cities, Pennsylvania, September 1987 : %

	Land tax rate	Building tax rate
Scranton	4.375	0.8
Harrisburg	5.525	2.188
McKeesport	9.0	2.0
New Castle	4.0	2.28
Duquesne	6.36	2.7
Washington	6.056	1.68
Pittsburgh	15.15	2.7

A study of Pittsburgh's dual-rate property tax concluded that a 1% decrease in the tax on buildings results in a 2.36% increase in the amount of new housing constructed in the city (Bourassa 1987).

4   Another feature of the Danish experience is worth noting, from the point of view of the cost of instituting an initial nationwide assessment. Valuers are recruited locally by the municipality to supplement the work of the taxation authorities' professional staff. The local valuers are selected from members of local political party organisations, and the composition of the valuation committees is largely a reflection of the local political party structure. According to the valuation law, no specific training or experience is required. When appointed, new members of the valuation committees are given introductory training, organised by the Inland Revenue. The job of local valuer is normally a sideline occupation; the fee received for a general valuation is about 10% of a skilled worker's annual income. This explains why the computerization of the valuation process in 1981, which reduced the number of valuers who had to be engaged locally, was not perceived as a threat against the vital interests of the professional groups. In spite of the reduction in their number, local valuers have welcomed the computerization, which executes the trivial, routine calculations. This has left them free to concentrate on applying their specialised, local knowledge on a few types of properties.

Hector Wilks, the London surveyor who undertook the valuation of every site in Whitstable on behalf of the Land Institute, employed unskilled assistants in the project, without detriment to the final result. This approach could be adopted for a fast and economical survey of the value of land in Britain, without loss of efficiency.

APPENDIX 1

The Relationship Between Commercial and Industrial Land Values

SHOP AND OFFICE buidings of similar quality command such varied rents and prices, even at the local level, that the value of commercial land has proved intractable to generalisation at the regional and national levels.

This fact is recognised in the Inland Revenue Valuation Office's *Property Market Report* which, according to the preface of the Autumn 1985 issue, 'incorporates views and records information about the property market from the 160 District Valuers throughout England and Wales', and, in the words of the Chief Valuer, has 'access to an unequalled pool from which to draw for independent analysis and informed comment on all aspects of the property market.' This six-monthly Report therefore contains charts summarising the regional distribution of land values in the residential, industrial and agricultural sectors. Yet it is unable to provide one for commercial land. The reasons for this are given on page 29:

> District Valuers are asked to comment generally on the activity in and market for land for office and shop development in their areas. This is perhaps the most difficult of all questions to answer. Sites are rarely purchased clearly. Rather, they tend to be an assemblage of various interests and ownerships acquired over possibly lengthy periods.
>
> Attempts to identify meaningful prices to try and establish patterns and trends for the purposes of this report have long since been abandoned. It might in any case be argued that land does not have a value, merely a price that is scheme specific and even peculiar to a particular developer.

Whatever the view of the Valuation Office this study could not refrain from attempting to place an aggregate value on commercial land simply because of the difficulty of the task. Its returns are no different in kind from those of other sites, so the asset value of British land would be incomplete without it.

One way to tackle the problem was to judge the multiple by which the value of a hectare of commercial land on average exceeds the value of a hectare of industrial land, and then to proceed from the regional averages for the latter to posit the regional averages for the former.

Evidence for this relationship was published in the *Property Market Report*. The Central Statistical Office commissioned a sample survey by District Valuers of industrial and commercial property values in England and Wales as at December 31, 1985. The summarised results appeared in the Spring issue for 1987. We argue in Chapter 8 that the site value findings are a considerable under-estimate. What matters for our present purpose, however, is the extent to which the under-estimate varied between sectors.

The main reasons for thinking that there was variation are the surprising facts that the survey found "little variation" in the proportion of site value to site and buildings value between different types of buildings, and that nevertheless it found the proportion for factories and mills (35.9%) to be greater than the overall average (31%). One would expect the proportion to be larger in the commercial than the industrial sector because it occupies relatively central, high value locations without containing buildings of comparable greater value. Offices, it is true, are at least twice as expensive per square metre as shops, factories and warehouses to build, and contain more floorspace per hectare, but they are also particularly prone to depreciation.

Two factors may account for the unexpectedly low values put on commercial sites. First, the degree of obsolescence of many office buildings may have been under-estimated — this is commonly the case, according to recent research — which lowers their site value residuals. Second, the requirement to value sites at existing use rather than full development use may have been more limiting in the commercial sector, where the scope for achieving high land values is much greater.

Supporting evidence for a higher multiple between commercial and industrial values than implied by the DV survey comes from the CSO's own tentative calculations (see Chapter 8) and the Whitstable Site Value Rating survey. In the former, the aggregate land value of private sector non-residential buildings and civil engineering works in the UK in 1985 was calculated as 35.6% of the combined value of land and buildings by subtracting capital stock estimates from balance sheet valuations. This proportion was higher than in the DV survey despite including Scotland and Northern Ireland, which would certainly have lowered it, and also North Sea oil and gas installations, which were counted as having no land value at all. Differences in treatment of depreciation are unlikely to explain the difference as the capital stock estimates assume remarkably long economic lives for buildings.

In the Whitstable survey the aggregate annual rental value in February 1973 of land used for commercial purposes was found to be 15% greater than the aggregate annual rental value in mid-1972 of commercial land and buildings together as indicated by the revaluation for normal rating purposes (The Land Institute 1974: 25). For industrial sites, however, the former was found to be just less than half of the latter. Both sectors in the town were considered to have 'depressed land values' at the time, and commercial land values had not risen dramatically in the intervening months. It is therefore clear that the land value proportion of property values was much greater in the commercial sector.

These lines of evidence justify us in assuming a greater commercial site value total than that recorded in the DV survey. Subtracting the survey's £44bn capital value of factories, mills and warehouses, excluding rateable plant and equipment, from the grand commercial and industrial total of £173bn leaves £129bn for the capital value of commercial property. Assuming that factories and warehouses had 36% of their value in their sites, the aggregate industrial site value was £15.84bn. Assuming also that commercial properties on average had 45% of their value in their sites (increasing the survey's finding by just over 50%), the aggregate site value becomes £58.05bn. Applying the areas of land calculated for each sector in Chapter 4 (Table 4: VII), 93,000 ha and 40,050 ha respectively, we find that industrial land was worth on average £170,000/

ha and commercial land £1.449m/ha, giving a ratio of 1 to 8.5.[1]

As a check, if we were to divide the rough site value totals of shops, offices and restaurants (£46.5bn) and of factories and covered warehouses (£15.84bn) by the available floorspace figures (132mm² and 369mm² respectively) we would expect to find a smaller multiple, other things being equal, because the office area is greater relative to the industrial area due to its being multi-storey. However, the ratio is still 1 to 8.2.

Assuming there is a discrepancy to explain, and that the floor-space statistics are essentially accurate, this suggests that either the commercial acreage was over-estimated (deflating unit values) or the industrial acreage under-estimated (inflating unit values), and that, either way, the industrial to commercial land value multiplier should be greater. If the former is the case then the commercial land value aggregate calculated would not be affected anyway; if the latter, then it would be an under-estimate (as would the industrial aggregate). So it seems safe to conclude that using this method the commercial and industrial land value of Great Britain can only be exaggerated if the regional industrial values to which the ratio is applied are too high, or if the industrial and commercial site value totals are misaligned.

For industrial land values we must rely on the accuracy of Table 7:IV. This produces a mean value almost two-thirds greater than the value derived from the DV survey. This may well measure the shortfall between existing use values and full development values in the industrial sector.

As for the sectoral alignment, the oft-quoted pioneering survey by Vallis may at first sight appear to cast some doubt upon it. Using the year books of the Estate Exchange and auction results published by *The Estates Gazette*, Vallis charted the trend of urban land values in England from 1892 to 1969 for each of three sectors. He found that in the mid 1960s — when the gap between the two was certainly smaller — the ratio of the median values recorded for industrial and commercial land was 1 to 21 (£27,500/ha to £576,000/ha). Unless the sector area figures used above are nowhere near the truth, then this flatly contradicts the CSO's findings.

In this matter, however, it is certainly Vallis's results which are far less reliable. The total number of industrial and commercial land transactions used in the survey was 1,025 spread out over 77 years, as opposed to 2,600 properties valued by District Valuers concentrating on one day. 638 industrial land transactions were recorded (half in the 1960s), 25% of which were in Greater London and a further 30% in the South East. 387 commercial land transactions were recorded (one-tenth in the 1960s), 73% of which were in Greater London and a further 11% in the South East. Quite clearly the English median value for commercial land was an inflated one (35% of observations were actually in central London), whereas the industrial median was far more representative of England as a whole (only 1% of observations were in central London). Vallis admitted that the overall bias towards London and the South East 'is a weakness of the survey, but the available data made it unavoidable'.

By contrast, the CSO was able to 'ensure a regional mix of properties in line with the distribution of industrial and commercial property throughout England and Wales'. This involved valuing 800 factories and 1,800 commercial buildings in 100 DV areas. It was not a scientific random sample but it was far less constrained than Vallis's.

The most comprehensive survey of property values is that undertaken for rating purposes by the District Valuers. However, this assesses annual rental values of land and buildings together, so even if an up-to-date valuation were available nothing more could be learnt from it without a survey of capital and site values as well. In the CSO-commissioned survey, therefore, the District Valuers have provided us with as much information as we can hope for in the absence of a more comprehensive national land valuation.

The rule of thumb that we have established of a 1 to 8.5 ratio between average industrial and commercial land values may be taken as applying at the national level — the level at which it was calculated — but we would not expect it to apply at the regional and district levels as well. The Cities of London and Westminster undoubtedly contain a disproportionate share of the nation's commercial land value, so we must look more closely at the prices which apply there.

The only direct evidence contained in the *Property Market Reports* comes from the Autumn 1986 issue in an article by the

Kensington and Chelsea District Valuer entitled 'The Changing
Face of Kensington High Street'. It states that 'the old Town
Hall was sold by the Royal Borough in July 1984 for £5.3m
(£38.5m/ha). It achieved notoriety when a demolition gang moved
in overnight just before a listing notice was due to be served by the
GLC ... The current record for the High Street [is] held by one of
the four shop units in the new development ... where a rent of
£930/m^2 in terms of Zone A, (Zone A depth 9.1m) was obtained at
the end of last year'. Apart from the four ground floor shops the
redevelopment included three floors of offices, which 'have recently been let at a rental of £180/m^2'.

The borough borders the west side of the City of Westminster
and is situated on the ridge of high office rents which continues
westwards along the M4. The prime rents cited were about half
those current at the peak of the ridge at its eastern end in the City of
London. The peak rents in Westminster, in the Mayfair and St.
James' areas, would have been about one-third greater than those in
Kensington. As for shops, the peak rent cited was about half the
peak level in Westminster, at the western end of Oxford Street.

As the buildings themselves do not vary much in value they tend
to be an equalising influence upon rents. The underlying sites must
therefore vary in value more than the values of the sites and
buildings together quoted above. Taking the £40m/ha site value of
Kensington Town Hall (which allows for demolition) suggests that
peak commercial land values in Westminster were, say £100m/ha,
and in the City, say, £160m/ha. Translating these peaks into
averages requires guesswork, so let us assume that the averages
outside the City of London were one-third the peak, and inside, in
view of the more uniform intensity of development, two-thirds the
peak. This means that average land values in Westminster were
about £33m/ha, and in the City about £106m/ha.

Confirmation of the figure for the City may be gained by the
residual method of valuation. We have sounder figures here on
which to base our calculations than we have for the rest of the
country. The City planners impose a 4-to-1 plot ratio on new
developments, which means that generally they cannot rise above
four storeys. We also know from the City planners that building
costs are in the region of £1,200/m^2 gross internal floor area,

including air conditioning. And we know fairly accurately from the Hillier Parker *City of London Office Rent Contour Map* for September 1985 that average rents were about £270/m² effective (net) area. So a hypothetical hectare (10,000m²) of modern office structure with 85% effective plan area would have rented for £9.18m p.a.

Investment yields along the £270/m² contour line were about 6%, according to the Autumn 1985 *PMR* (Dawson House on Jewry Street, just inside the contour, was reported as purchased at an initial yield of 5.75% compared with 4.75% for prime City yields and a 6.41% value weighted average yield for Inner London). The capitalised value of the structure would therefore have been £153m. The cost of building the structure would have approached £48m. This suggests a capital value for the hectare site of about £105m. That is near enough the number we originally calculated.

NOTES

1   It might be argued, looking at Table 8:IX, that the industrial land area has been relatively over-stated for the purposes of this calculation (which excludes vacant land). However, this possibility is unlikely. It is more probable that the industrial area in Table 4:VII has been under-stated, and/or the developable but vacant industrial land belongs in the category 'Some mineral workings/dereliction', which has also been under-stated. The figure for the latter (20,000 ha) is notional, because in none of the land use surveys consulted was this area separately identified. Waste land as a whole forms an indeterminate category straddling both urban and rural definitions. The Second Land Utilisation Survey deals with it more specifically than the others, and the treatment suggests that much urban wasteland lies outside the 'settlement supercategory'. Its *Field Mapping Manual* states that 'Derelict land may develop into reverted land if it is left long enough for vegetative growth to obliterate all traces of masonry, paving or quarry outcrops' (Coleman and Shaw 1980:56). Derelict land is classified as settlement; reverted, or 'rough land', is not. 178,000 ha of rough land was recorded in England and Wales in the 1963 survey, a substantial proportion of which must have been vacant urban land. None of this land is included in column 1 of Table 4:II, nor therefore in Table 4:VII.

The Evidence of Rateable Values

IN APPENDIX 1 it was suggested that current rateable values are not useful for indicating land rents because they are not regularly updated and because they are assessed on land and buildings together. In this appendix we attempt to up-date British rateable values in the light of the Scottish revaluation of 1st April 1985. We then capitalise the resulting net property rents and apply to them the site value proportions of capital values used in Appendix 1. Finally, we compare the resulting ratios between the land value totals of the sectors with the ratios obtained in this study.

The results of the Scottish revaluation (Table A2 : I) represented the effect of the changes in property values between 1976 and 1983 on the total values of the property that existed in 1985. For England and Wales we need to know the effect of the changes in property values between mid-1972 (the effective date of the 1973 revaluation) and mid-1985 on the total values of the property that existed in 1985.

We may take the Scottish changes as fairly typical of British changes from 1976 to 1983. Scotland's share of UK GDP (excluding the continental shelf) fell from 9.1% to 9.0% in this period. Scottish average house prices increased slightly more slowly than the UK average (2.1 times as opposed to 2.34 times, according to the Nationwide Building Society). Scottish office and shop prime rents almost kept up with the GB average from 1977 to 1983, according to Healey & Baker's *PRIME* report. Industrial rents lagged over the whole of Britain.

According to the Nationwide, UK average house prices increased 4.5 times from 1972 to 1985, and by exactly half that multiple from 1976 to 1983. So let us assume *all* unit net annual

Table A2 : I
Scottish rateable values (net annual values)
before and after the 1985 revaluation

| | 1st April 1984 (at 1st July 1976 values) | | 1st April 1985 (at 1st July 1983 values) | |
	£m	%	£m	%
Domestic	489	33.9	1,301	40.3
Industrial, freight transport subjects, public utilities	335*	23.2	592*	18.3
Commercial	374	25.9	841	26.1
Miscellaneous	245	17.0	493	15.3
	1,443	100.0	3,227	100.0

* A deduction of 10% has been made for the value of rated plant and equipment (see Bryant 1987:114). Industrial re-rating (50% in 1984 and 40% in 1985) has been removed.

Source: Scottish Office.

values in England & Wales in this period increased twice as much as they increased in Scotland between 1976 and 1983. Scottish average house prices increased by about 15% from 1983 to 1985, so let us assume that all Scottish unit rateable values increased by that proportion in that period. The British values may then be calculated, as in Table A2:II.

Converting the net annual values to their capital equivalents using the 1985 yields adopted by this study (see Table 2:I) produces the capital values in column (1) of Table A2:III.

The equivalent land values produced by this study (deducting the vacant land values of Table 8:IX from the sectoral totals of Table 2:I — but see footnote in Appendix 1 — and deducting a further 1% for the value of building sites — see Bryant 1987: 114) are as in column (2) of the table.

It may seem implausible that the values for land should be almost as high as the values for land and buildings together. But the latter are based on 'net annual values', which assume that the tenant has the responsibility for all repairs and insurance. Such values are

Table A2 : II
Scottish rates of change applied to Britain

England and Wales	1st April 1985 (at mid-1972 values)		Increase	1st April 1985 (at mid-1985 values)	
	£m	%	Factor	£m	%
Domestic	3,815	49.8	5.32	20,296	56.6
Industrial, warehousing, public utilities	1,426*	18.6	3.53	5,034	14.0
Commercial	1,720	22.4	4.5	7,740	21.6
Miscellaneous	703	9.2	4	2,812	7.8
	7,664	100.0		35,882	100.0
Great Britain					
Domestic				21,792	55.0
Industrial, warehousing, public utilities				5,715	14.4
Commercial				8,707	22.0
Miscellaneous				3,379	8.5
				39,593	100.0

* A deduction of 10% has been made as in Table A2:I.

Source: Inland Revenue (1986:78).

considerably lower than the gross rental values upon which market capital values may be based. Also they are existing development values, whereas the values for sites are full development values.

We cannot say, therefore, to what extent rateable values confirm the absolute findings of this study. But there is no reason why they should not be used as a check on the relative positions of the sectors.

The value of occupied residential land in this study comprises 35% of the total value of British housing in the CSO balance sheet. In Appendix 1 we took 36% and 45% as the proportions of land value in occupied industrial and commercial property, respectively, in England and Wales. These latter proportions would be slightly

Table A2 : III
Relative capital values for the sectors of Britain (£bn)

	(1) *Net annual values capitalised*	(2) *Land values from this study*	(3) *Land values from rates ratios*
Domestic	272.4	239.7	239.7
Commercial	108.8	103.8	120.5
Industrial, warehousing, public utilities	45.7	28.4	40.3

high for Britain because the Scottish figures would be considerably lower than the average for England and Wales. Reducing them to 35% and 44% produces the following land value ratios between the sectors: housing to commerce, 1.99 to 1; commerce to industry, 2.99 to 1.

The soundest data available to this study were for the value of residential land, and we are fairly confident of our estimate for this sector. Applying the ratios to that estimate in column (2) of Table A2:III produces the commercial and industrial land value aggregates in column (3). These very broadly confirm the relative positions of the sectors in column (2), though they do indicate that the commercial and industrial totals may have been under-estimated by this study.

PART THREE

11
Land Valuation and Fiscal Policy in Denmark

ANDERS MÜLLER AND
GREGERS MØRCH-LASSEN
Inland Revenue Directorate, Copenhagen

IN DENMARK the total market value of land can be estimated quite accurately. Table 11 : I shows the value of different types of land for 1986. The total is 385 milliard Dkr. (£1.00 = 11.40 Dkr.). The figures are the result of a process of public valuation which takes place every four years. For each property the land is valued at the highest and best economic use, disregarding the existing buildings. The land value includes site improvements like drainage, sewerage and roads.

For all urban and recreational land the valuation is very accurate. Agricultural land, however, is undervalued due to the regulations which determine the valuation of this type of land. The public valuation includes 97% of all land and only excludes roads, railways, airports, seaports, churches, parks and defence installations.

Adjusting for the under-valuation of agricultural land and for the value of land not included in the public valuation, the total market value of all land in Denmark can be estimated as 450 milliard Dkr. for the year 1986. The market value of all real estate (land and buildings) was 1,500 milliard Dkr. The national income for 1986 was 580 milliard Dkr., and a rough estimate of the value of all assets is 2,000 milliard Dkr.

Table 11 : I
Market value of land, 1986

Type of land	Area (km²) '000s	Value (million Dkr)
Residential	1,300	208,863
Commercial	62	12,971
Mixed commercial and residential	171	21,943
Industrial	189	13,313
Public administration	617	24,536
Private institutions, etc	93	4,775
Recreational[1]	380	20,359
Vacant urban land	640	20,237
Agriculture	33,158	45,210
Woods	3,664	2,377
Miscellaneous	914	11,235
Total	41,188	385,819

1 Summer houses and week-end cabins.

£1 = 11.40 Dkr.

Public Valuations

Taxes related to properties have been important in Denmark for centuries, as has been the case in many other countries. To establish a fair and equitable base for taxation the market value of all properties has been assessed every four years since 1903. Since 1920, when a land tax was introduced, the capital value of the land has also been assessed every four years. Both the land value and the total value are capital values and not annual or rental values. Table 11 : II shows the overall result of the valuations since 1926.

The values are used for all the different taxes related to the properties, and for a number of other purposes as well (payment for water, garbage removal and road maintenance, calculation of grants to municipalities and appreciation of buildings for business).

Valuation is carried out by the central government with secretarial assistance from the municipalities. Both for central govern-

Table 11 : II
The value of real estate, 1926-1986

	Land value (milliard Dkr)	Total value (milliard Dkr)
1927	5.1	13.2
1932	5.0	13.7
1936	5.6	15.7
1945	6.8	20.8
1950	9.3	29.5
1956	12.5	47.1
1960	17.2	68.4
1965	41.2	150.0
1969	67.4	242.9
1973	103.5	397.7
1977	194.3	769.5
1981	319.8	1,115.1
1981[1]	229.7	800.6
1986[1]	385.8	1,461.7

1 Cash equivalent value (before 1981 valuation based on nominal value; that is, equivalent to the amount written in the deed.)

ment and the municipalities the valuation administration is a part of the general tax administration.[1]

The valuation is based on the basic information about each property, that is, the size, quality and location of the land, and the size, age, installations and material used for the building. The valuation is also based on the collected information about the sales prices of all sold properties, the planning regulations and the knowledge of the local valuer.

Valuation Standards

Two values are assessed for each property:

— Total value (land and buildings)
— Land value

The *total value* is the full market value of the property including land and buildings but excluding machinery, furniture and livestock. The value is the average *cash* payment a sensible buyer would pay for the property at the time of valuation.

The basis of the valuation is the best economic use to which the property can be put. All public rules and regulations — like planning regulations, preservation of buildings or nature and rent control — must be taken into consideration. Private regulation and agreements are not taken into account. That means that unusual rent agreements or special mortgage conditions do not influence the value.

The *land value* must be the full market value (assuming cash payment) of the land without the buildings. The best economic use of the land — disregarding the existing buildings and the present land use — is the basis of the valuation. All public regulations concerning the land — but not the buildings — are taken into consideration.

Land in rural zones is assessed at the best economic use for agriculture. The value depends on the basic agricultural quality of the land and of the location in relation to the market outlet for agricultural products. An average condition concerning fertilizer, marling etc. is assumed. On the market the price per hectare of agricultural land also depends on the size of the farm, but this element is disregarded in the valuation. The value of an expected transfer of the land to the urban zone is also disregarded, but this value is included in the total value of the property.

The land value includes site improvements like drainage, sewerage and roads. However, a special assessment of an owner's actual costs for site improvements can be made and can be deducted from the taxable land value for 30 years.

Valuation Techniques

Land valuation in urban areas is primarily based on statistical analysis of sales of vacant land (plots). The annual number of sales are between 4,000 and 6,000. Only arm's-length transactions in the open market are considered. For each type of land, sales statistics indicate land value. Different factors influence different types of land. Simple models explaining the price structure have been developed for each type of land.

For land intended for apartment houses or commercial buildings the price of land depends on the total floor space which can be constructed on a plot. Besides location and size of plot, permitted building/land ratio according to planning regulations is the decisive factor influencing the price. In areas intended for apartment houses or commercial activities, sale prices of vacant land are related to permitted building/land ratio according to planning regulations.

Sales of vacant land will often be located on the periphery of urban areas. In densely built-up areas only a few sales are recorded. The valuation authorities therefore include sales of other types of properties in order correctly to estimate the land value. A variety of techniques are used in this process.

— Sales of single-family houses, terrace houses and summer-houses: the computer models used for estimation of the total value of these properties produce statistics which can be used to indicate general land value levels in different regions of the country.

— Analyses of sales of properties with demolished buildings. On the sales report the buyer must indicate if he intends to demolish existing buildings. The land value is calculated by deducting the average demolition cost from the sale price. In some city areas this will be the only approach available. The number of sales of this kind are quite substantial. In the Copenhagen area 100 sales were recorded during the 4-year period prior to the 1986 valuation.

— Using the knowledge of the valuer. Local valuation commit-tees have knowledge about the structure of land values in their valuation circle. With the use of that experience, land values in densely built-up areas can be calculated from the sale prices of plots in inferior locations.

Practical valuation involves a combination of all methods. The definition of land value has implications which seem odd to the public but are logical. If utilisation of land is inefficient according to planning regulations (for instance, if a single-family house is located in an area where regulations permit commercial activities) land value exceeds total value. Following the 1986 valuation, this was found to be the case for approximately 1,500 properties.

Ownership has no influence whatsoever on land value (or total value). The best economic use decides the valuation. A government building and a private office building will have identical land values if size of plot, location and planning regulations are identical.

The valuation of agricultural land is different from the valuation of urban land. The basis is the classification of all agricultural land according to productive quality. Before each valuation a number of sold agricultural properties are selected and visited by experts from the Danish Inland Revenue and The National Tax Board. After each visit the sales price is analysed and divided into three parts:

— value of production buildings

— value of residence, and

— value of land.

Using the results from these visits (200 by the 1986 valuation), The National Tax Board decides on values for agricultural land of medium quality located in 10 different regions. With that as a basis, the value of land of all the other qualities is calculated.

Computer Assistance

During the period 1960-1980 computer registers were established which contained all the basic information needed for the valuation. Two very powerful valuation systems were established for the 1981 valuation and expanded for the 1986 valuation.

The Land Value System calculates the land value of all properties. As a basis for this the detailed planning regulations are recorded for all areas, and land value areas are formed each having only one type of permitted land use. For each land value area a 'price' or an updating factor is reported. The land value can then be calculated for each property using different mathematical models for different types of permitted land use.

The Total Value System calculates the total value for single-family houses, two and three-family houses, summer houses, freehold flats and rental multi-family houses. The basis is statistical analysis of the sold properties resulting in different mathematical models for each type of property. The value of the building is then calculated and the land value is added.

Since 1982 there has been a computer update of all values for the years between valuations. The update is based on the price trend for different types of properties in different areas.

The valuation systems do not replace the human judgement in the valuation process. They do, however, execute a vast number of calculations and recordings which previously had to be performed by the local valuers. For this reason the number of local valuers was reduced in 1982 from 3,840 to 1,444. This has reduced the total cost of the valuation administration by approximately 50 million Dkr. Table 11:III shows the different taxes related to properties in Denmark.

The Property Tax is a local tax levied by both the municipalities and the counties. Ninety per cent of the revenue is a land tax based on the assessed capital land value for each property. Almost all types of properties are subject to the land tax including vacant plots and agricultural land. Ten per cent of the revenue is tax on the value of buildings used for business and publicly-owned buildings.

Table 11 : III
Taxes related to properties, 1985
(million Dkr)

	Total tax	*Tax of properties*
Property tax	5,600	5,600
Income tax of imputed rentals	6,000	6,000
Development gains tax	40	40
Property transfer tax	900	900
Net wealth tax	1,300	520
Inheritance and gift duty	1,400	500
Capital gains tax	1,700	100
Total	—	13,660
Per cent of total taxes and duties	—	4.5%
Per cent of GDP	—	2.2%

Owner-occupiers of dwellings and summer homes must include an imputed rental value of the property in their personal income for the income tax. The imputed rental is a percentage of the total capital value of the property.

When rural land is redesignated as urban land, the owner must pay development gain tax, which is half the increase in assessed land value due to the re-zoning.

When properties are sold or transferred, a property transfer tax (or stamp duty) must be paid to the Land Registry. The tax is 1.2% of the sales price or the assessed value, whichever is the higher.

Table 11:III further shows how much of the revenue of net wealth tax, inheritance and gift duty and capital gains tax can be attributed to properties.

Costs of Valuation

The total costs of valuation and collection of property taxes have been estimated as 260 million Dkr. for 1986, when valuation took place, and 200 million Dkr. for the years before and after. The costs are related to data-processing maintenance of the computer registers, all costs of personnel and honoraria for the local valuers. The costs are only 1.5-2.0% of the revenue.

NOTES

1   The local valuers are appointed by the municipality (4-8 per valuation circle). They are exclusively recruited from members of local political party organizations and the composition of the valuation committees is by and large a reflection of the local political party structure. According to the valuation law no specific training or experience is required. When appointed, new members of the valuation committees receive introductory training organized by the Inland Revenue.

The job as local valuer is a typical sideline occupation. That explains why the computerization of the valuation process was not conceived as a threat against the vital interests of any professional group. In spite of the reduction in number, the local valuers have welcomed the computerization because they can concentrate on a few types of properties. Trivial routine calculations are done by the computers, which offers the local valuers a great opportunity to apply their special knowledge in the valuation process.

12

Rental Income in the USA: Mystery of the Missing Billions

FRED E. FOLDVARY

A STUDY by Steven Cord, who at the time was professor of history at Indiana University, Pennsylvania, concluded that the annual economic rent of land in 1981 was about $650 bn, or 28% of the national income (Cord 1985: 279). His calculations were based on data from the US Bureau of the Census and the Federal Reserve Board.

The economic rent of British land in 1985 is estimated to be equivalent to 22.4% of national income. Had this study used a uniform interest rate a couple of percentage points below home loan mortgage rates for converting all capital values into rental values, as Cord's study did, the land rent to national income ratios would be about equal. Yet in both countries, especially in the USA, official reporting of rental income gives no indication that land rent might play a significant part in the economy.

In the *United Kingdom National Accounts*, which include Northern Ireland as well as Great Britain, published by the Central Statistical Office, gross rental incomes in 1985 (i.e. before capital consumption), including imputed charges for capital consumption of non-trading capital and imputed incomes from owner-occupied homes, amounted to 9.2% of national income. 65% of this was in the personal sector, and 64% was imputed. Net rental incomes (after capital consumption) could not have been more than 4.5% of national income, but adding government revenue from the North Sea as a measure of oil rents brings the proportion back to 9%. This figure does not include imputed rents for owner-occupied properties other than homes, but it does encompass the rents of buildings and permanent improvements as well as land.

In the United States, official statistics at first glance indicate that the rent of land might be even less significant. The rental income of land and buildings is calculated by the Bureau of Economic Analysis, US Department of Commerce, and reported in *The Survey of Current Business* (SCB) and *Economic Indicators* (both Washington, DC, USPGO). But it is for the personal sector only, including imputed rents for owner-occupied dwellings.

The calculation has undergone two major changes. Beginning with the January 1976 issue of the SCB, a capital consumption adjustment was subtracted from gross rental income. The data for several previous years was recalculated, but data calculated by the previous method is not comparable. The older figures were from 10% to 20% higher than the new ones.

An even greater revision was introduced in the December 1985 issue of the SCB (p.11). Revised figures for the series are given in the February 1986 issue (p.24). This series has allegedly 'improved accounting for expenses of home ownership', which drastically reduces reported rental income. However, the annual revisions downwards are not proportionate but vary erratically, as the latest revised list shows in Table 12 : I. The estimate of personal net rental income for 1981 was 0.6% of national income.

Table 12 : I
Rental income of persons in the USA
($ billion)

	1976 basis	1985 basis
1981	42.3	13.3
1982	51.5	13.6
1983	58.3	13.2
1984	62.5	8.5

A break down of personal rental income was provided in Table 6 of the July 1988 issue of SCB, and we give the 1986 figures in Table 12 : II.

Table 12 : II
Breakdown of rental income of persons in the USA, 1986
($ billion)

Oil royalties	8.6
Farms	5.1
Nonfarm nonresidential	8.0
Nonfarm housing	35.8
Gross rental income	57.4
minus Capital consumption	− 45.0
Net rental income	12.4

Note: Numbers do not add up due to rounding.

The December 1985 SCB classified the revisions as 'definitional', 'capitalize residential replacements', and 'statistical' (p.11). The latter was the major change. In 1984, for example, it consisted of a 'statistical' subtraction of $55.9 bn. In the description of the changes on the same page, the SCB stated that 'The revision lowers the level of rental income of persons by substantial amounts throughout the 1970s and 1980s.' This was due primarily to two statistical changes — an expanded list of homeownership expenses, and the incorporation of data from the Census of Housing, lowering the estimate of 'space rent' from 1973 onwards.

'Space rent,' also called 'gross housing product,' is calculated by the US Department of Commerce and published in the SCB and in the *Statistical Abstract of the United States* (Washington, DC, USPGO)). It measures personal consumption of housing as the gross rental value of real estate before deducting expenses and depreciation, less expenditures for transient dwellings such as hotels. Theoretically, it should be proportional to net rental income, but it is not proportional to the 1985-revised series.

From Table 12:III we must conclude that the 1985-revised figures for rental income have little economic significance. Between 1960 and 1985, with gross national product growing, the value of the dollar decreasing, and the housing stock increasing, we would

Table 12 : III
Net rental income of persons in the USA, 1985 — revised series ($ billion)

1960	1970	1979	1986
15.3	18.2	5.6	12.4

expect the income from real estate to grow proportionately: instead, it *shrank* according to the figures. Between 1970 and 1986 the population grew by almost 20% from 203 million, and residential capital (given in the SCB) in constant dollars increased by 56%, yet rental income divided by the GNP deflator (1982 = 100) is estimated to have fallen from $38.6 bn to $10.9 bn. How real rental income could have declined by 72% while residential capital increased by 56% is an intriguing question.

Real estate is a major component of national wealth and income. In 1985, residences in the US were valued at $3,502 bn, 32% of the total stock of tangible wealth (*Statistical Abstract*, 1986-87, Table 754), yet rental income was put at $9.2 bn (SCB July 1988, p. 45).

The lack of credibility of the rental income data, especially the current series, has important consequences. Rent is a component of the national income, so if it is being understated the national income is also being understated, unless rental income has been shifted to some other category. Could the expenses of housing have risen so much that they absorb most of the annual income of real estate?

Much of what is reported as interest and dividends in the national income is actually rental income. Mortgage payments to banks, net of overheads, are in turn paid to depositors and investors as interest and dividends. But it is not clear that the missing rental income has artificially boosted these categories as reported in the national income accounts.

A second problem, if rent is being understated, may be the effect on economics as a science. Economists today typically relegate rent to a minor role in the modern economy. Paul A. Samuelson, in his textbook *Economics*, assures students that 'historically, pure land

rent has become a declining fraction of GNP and NNP ...'
(1980 : 684n). Certainly, if one believes the national income
accounts, one gets this impression. But the studies by Cord and the
authors of this book prove otherwise. Also, a study by Allen
Manvel in 1968 estimated the land value component of US real
estate as about 41% (Cord 1985 : 281). Even gross housing product,
combining tenant and owner-occupied housing, land and buildings
($279 bn in 1981), plus corporate and government rent, might not
cover Cord's net rent figure for land alone (about $540 bn in 1981,
apart from mineral rents and local property taxes).

This leaves a large gap for research. The question is: is any
economic rent missing? If so, where did it go?

This also leads to a third consideration, the public choice issue. If
the calculation and publication of statistics is subject to the same
types of political influences as other government activities, it would
be theoretically possible that the low figures for rental income are
due to 'rent-seeking' in the literal meaning of that term. Low
figures give rental income a low profile and would help minimize
the taxation of rent and real estate. Favourable tax legislation
would let the owners of real estate keep more of their rents. The
fact that both the revisions of the rental income series have been in a
downward direction, and that the second revision reports rental
income as decreasing while the economy as a whole was expanding,
is consistent with such a public choice hypothesis.

The mystery of the missing rent awaits resolution.

Bibliography

Aganbegyan, Abel (1988), *The Challenge: Economics of Perestroika*, London: Hutchinson.

Agriculture EDC (1987), *Directions for Change: Land Use in the 1990s*, London: NEDO

Arnold, Arthur (1880), *Free Land*, London: Kegan Paul.

Association of Metropolitan Authorities/Association of District Councils (1988), 'Costs of Poll Tax Soar', Press Release 74/88, May 15

Audit Commission (1988), *Local Authority Property – A Management Overview*, London: HMSO.

Banham, J. M. M. (1986), Letter to Mr. M. Fisher, Whale Tankers Ltd, Solihull, June 12.

Best, R. H. (1981), *Land Use and Living Space*, London: Methuen.

Best, R. H. and Anderson, M. (1984), 'Land-Use Structure and Change in Britain, 1971 to 1981', *The Planner*, November.

Bidney, David (1946), 'The Concept of Cultural Crisis', *American Anthropologist*, N. S., 48.

— (1947), 'Cultural Theory and the Problems of Cultural Crises', in L. Bryson, L. Finkelstein and R. M. MacIver, eds., *Approaches to Group Understanding*, Sixth Symposium, New York.

Binswanger, Hans (1988), *Fiscal and Legal Incentives with Environmental Effects on the Brazilian Amazon*, Washington, DC: World Bank Discussion paper 69.

Body, Richard (1982), *Agriculture: The Triumph and The Shame*, London: Temple Smith.

— (1987), *Red or Green for Farmers*, Saffron Walden: Broad Leys Publishing.

Bourassa, Steven C., (1987), 'Land Value Taxation and New Housing Development in Pittsburgh', *Growth and Change*, Vol. 18 (Fall: 44-56).

Bover, Olympia, John Muellbauer and Anthony Murphy (1988),

Housing, Wages and UK Labour Markets, London: Centre for Economic Policy Research.

British Gas Corporation (1986), *Annual Report and Accounts 1985-86,* London.

British Geological Survey (1987), Natural Environment Research Council, *U.K. Mineral Statistics 1987,* London: Keyworth.

Bruton, M. J., and Gore, A. (1980), *Vacant Urban Land in South Wales,* Cardiff: UWIST.

Bryant, C. G. E. (1987), 'National and Sector Balance Sheets 1957-1985', in *Economic Trends,* No. 403, London: HMSO, May.

BCIS (1986), *Quarterly Review of Building Prices,* London: RICS, February.

Cantell, T. (1977), *Urban Wasteland,* London: Civic Trust.

CSO (1985), *UK National Accounts: Sources and Methods,* London: HMSO, Third Edition.

CSO (1987a & 1988a), *Regional Trends 22 & 23,* London: HMSO.

CSO (1987 & 1988), *Social Trends 17 and 18,* London: HMSO.

Chisholm, M., and Kivell, P. (1987), *Inner City Waste Land: An Assessment of Government and Market Failure in Land Development.* London: IEA.

Chorley, Lord (1987), *Handling Geographic Information,* London: HMSO.

Civic Trust (1988), *Urban Wasteland Now,* London: Civic Trust.

Coleman, A. and Shaw, J. E. (1980), *Land Utilisation Survey: Field Mapping Manual,* London: King's College.

Committee of Public Accounts (1982), *Crown Estate Abstract Accounts 1980-1981,* London: HMSO, July 26.

Cord, Steven (1985), 'How Much Revenue Would a Full Land Value Tax Yield?' *Am. J. of Economics and Sociology,* Vol. 44, No. 3.

Deane, G. (1986), 'Statistics Measure Post-War Change', in *Town and Country Planning,* December.

Dept. of Energy (1986), *Development of the Oil and Gas Resources of the U.K. in 1985,* London: HMSO.

Dept. of the Environment (1978), *Developed Areas 1969: A Survey of England and Wales from Air Photography,* London: DoE.

Dept. of the Environment, Scottish Development Department and Welsh Office (1986), *Housing and Construction Statistics 1975-*

85 Great Britain. London: HMSO.

Dept. of the Environment (1986a), *Commercial and Industrial Floorspace Statistics; England 1982-85,* London: HMSO.

Dept. of the Environment (1986b), *Paying for Local Government,* London: HMSO.

Dept. of the Environment (1986 & 1987), 'Land Use Change in England', *Statistical Bulletin (86) 1 & (87) 7,* London: DoE.

Dept. of the Environment (1988), *Urban Land Markets in the UK,* London: HMSO.

Dickinson, G. C. and Shaw, M. G. (1982), 'Land Use in Leeds 1957-1976: Two Decades of Change in a British City', *Environment and Planning A.* Vol. 14.

Douglas, Roy (1976), *Land, People & Politics,* London: Alison & Busby.

Dowrick, F. E. (1974), 'Public Ownership of Land — Taking Stock 1972-73', *Public Law,* Spring.

Dwyer, T. M. (1982), 'Henry George's Thought in Relation to Modern Economics', *The Am. J. of Economics and Sociology,* Vol. 41, No. 4.

Estates Gazette, The (1987), 'Review 1986: Industrial', Supplement, January 17.

Evans, A.W. (1974), 'Private Sector Housing Land Prices in England and Wales', *Economic Trends,* 244, London: HMSO, February.

Financial Times (1987), 'International Coal Report', Issue No. 184, October 23.

Fenwick, A. T. (1987), letter to B. Mackenzie, January 20.

Fleming, M. C. (1986), *Spon's Guide to the Housing, Construction and Property Market Statistics,* London: Spon.

Fleming, M. C., and Nellis, J. G. (1987), *Spon's House Price Data Book.,* London: Spon.

Fordham, R. C. (1974), *Measurement of Urban Land Uses,* Occasional Paper No. 1, Cambridge: Department of Land Economy.

— (1975), 'Urban Land Use Change in the United Kingdom during the Second Half of the Twentieth Century', *Urban Studies* 12.

Fothergill, S., *et al.* (1985), *Urban Industrial Change,* DoE/DTI Inner Cities Research Programme, London: HMSO.

Gaffney, Mason (1982), 'Two Centuries of Economic Thought on Taxation of Land Rents', in Richard W. Lindholm and Arthur D. Lynn, Jr., eds, *Land Value Taxation*, Madison: University of Wisconsin Press.

— (1986), 'Land as a Distinctive Factor of Production', Notes: unpublished.

Garnaut, R., and Clunies Ross A. (1983), *Taxation of Mineral Resources*. Oxford: Clarenden Press.

Gilder, George (1981), *Wealth and Poverty*, New York: Basic Books.

Hall, P. C. (1987), 'The Industrial Revolution in Reverse', *Planning for a Surfeit of Land?* RICS & RTPI Conference, November 3.

Hallett, Graham (1979), *Urban Land Economics*, London: Macmillan.

Hardie, A. (1987), interview with C. G. E. Bryant on November 18.

Harrison, Fred (1983), *The Power in the Land*, London: Shepheard Walwyn.

— (1988), 'The Real State of Denmark', *Land and Liberty*, March-Apr.

Healey & Baker Research (1988), *PRIME Property Rent Indices and Market Editorial*, London: Healey & Baker, Summer.

Hobbes, T. (1651), *Leviathan.*

Hunting Surveys and Consultants Ltd., (1986), *Monitoring Landscape Change*, Bristol: Dept. of the Environment and Countryside Commission.

Inland Revenue (1987), *Inland Revenue Statistics 1986*, London: HMSO.

Inland Revenue Valuation Office, *Property Market Report*, London: Surveyors Publications, Six-monthly from 1983 (annual from 1988).

Inner City Commission (1987), *Private Housebuilding in the Inner Cities.* London: House Builders Federation, July.

Land Institute (1974), *Site Value Rating*, London.

Lawson, Nigel (1988), 'Why freedom has paid off', *The Sunday Times*, July 24.

Lean, Geoffrey (1988), 'Angry Ridley raps "selfish" Tory rebels', *The Observer*, May 15.

Lilley, Peter (1980), *North Sea Giveaway: The Case for Auctioning North Sea Oil Licences*, London: Bow Publications, 1980.

Lipsey, Richard (1979), *An Introduction to Positive Economics*, London: Weidenfeld and Nicolson, fifth edn.

MAFF 1974, *Agricultural Land Classification of England and Wales*, London: HMSO.

— 1986a, *Agricultural Land Prices in England and Wales in 1984/5*, London: MAFF.

— 1986b *Agricultural Statistics for the UK 1985*, London: HMSO.

— 1987a, *Farm Incomes in the UK*, London: HMSO.

— 1987b *MAFF Statistics, Current Agricultural Land Prices in England and Wales*, London: MAFF.

— 1987c *MAFF Statistics, Grass Keep Enquiry*, London: MAFF.

Moss, Graham (1981), *Britain's Wasting Acres*, London: Architectural Press.

National Audit Office (1988a), *Estate Management in the National Health Service*, London: HMSO.

National Audit Office (1988b), *The Crown Estate*, London: HMSO.

National Coal Board (1986), *Annual Report and Accounts 1985/6*, London.

OECD (1988), *Japan*, Paris: OECD

Pettigrew, C. W. (1980), 'National and Sector Balance Sheets for the UK', in *Economic Trends*, 325, London: HMSO, November.

Property Services Agency (1986), *Annual Report and Accounts for 1985-86*, London.

Rhind, D. and Hudson, R. (1980), *Land Use*, London: Methuen.

Samuelson, Paul (1976), *Economics*, Tokyo: McGraw-Hill Koga Kusha, 10th edn.

Samuelson, Paul, and William D. Nordhaus (1985), *Economics*, McGraw-Hill, 12th edn.

Schumpeter, J. A. (1954), *History of Economic Analysis*, New York: Oxford University Press.

Spencer, Peter (1988), *The Community Charge and its Likely Effects on the U.K. Economy*, London: Credit Suisse First Boston.

Stockman, David (1987), *The Triumph of Politics*, London: Coronet.

Treasury and Civil Service Committee (1988), *The 1988 Budget*,

London: HMSO, Fourth Report, April 20.

Vallis, E. A. (1972), 'Urban Land and Building Prices 1892-1969', *The Estates Gazette*, Vol. 222, May.

Walls, P. (1984), 'New DoE Land Use Surveys', *The Planner*, November.

Welsh Office (1986), *Commercial and Industrial Floorspace Statistics: Wales No. 7 1986*, Cardiff: Welsh Office.

About the Authors

Ronald Banks is a property developer and foreign exchange broker and was for 15 years a lecturer at the School of Economic Studies, London.

Fred E. Foldvary, BA, is carrying out his post-graduate research in public finance at George Mason University, Fairfax, Virginia.

Alexandra Rose Hardie, Ph.D., is a lecturer in economics at the University of Exeter.

Fred Harrison, M.Sc., is Director of the Centre for Incentive Taxation and author of *The Power in the Land* (1983).

Gregers Mørch-Lassen, MA, is engaged in the planning of the computer systems used for property valuation by Denmark's Inland Revenue Directorate.

John Loveless, M.Sc., is a lecturer in civil engineering at the University of Bristol who has written about urban wasteland for the Adam Smith Institute.

Anders Müller, MA, is the author of technical papers on computer-assisted land valuation presented at conferences of the International Real Estate Federation and the International Association of Assessing Officers.

Duncan W. Pickard, Ph.D., farms 70 acres in West Yorkshire and is lecturer in animal nutrition at the University of Leeds.

David Richards, MA, is Senior Researcher with the Economic and Social Science Research Association.

Francis M. Smith, Ph.D., formerly the Technical Director of a multinational chemical company, is a business consultant.

Index